Inventory credit

An approach to developing agricultural markets

FAO
AGRICULTURAL
SERVICES
BULLETIN

120

by
Jonathan Coulter
Natural Resources Institute
and
Andrew W. Shepherd
FAO

NATURAL
RESOURCES
INSTITUTE

Food
and
Agriculture
Organization
of
the
United
Nations

Rome, 1995

M-63
ISBN 92-5-103703-5

Preface

The last decade has seen a gradual trend towards the liberalization of many economies, both in the developing world of Africa, Asia and Latin America and, more recently, in Eastern Europe and the new states of the former Soviet Union.

An important feature of these changes has been the liberalization of agricultural markets. This has involved an increasing role for the private sector in food marketing and, to a lesser but nevertheless significant extent, in the marketing of export and industrial crops.

In most countries the lack of finance for private traders has emerged as a significant constraint to the emergence of a dynamic private sector able to take over the bulk of trading and storage functions from state trading bodies. The authors, and their colleagues in NRI and FAO, recognizing this constraint, identified inventory credit as constituting, at least in part, a useful approach to resolving the problem. Initially, our two organizations worked separately, but when it was realized that we were working along similar lines it was felt beneficial to collaborate on this publication.

Anthony Beattie
Chief Executive
Natural Resources Institute

Abdoulaye Sawadogo
Assistant Director-General
Agriculture Department
Food and Agriculture Organization

Contents

Acknowledgements

The authors acknowledge the many people and organizations who have assisted with this research. The contribution of Dr Edward Asante, of the Ghana Institute of Management and Public Administration, is particularly acknowledged with regard to the Ghana case study, as are the contributions of Jonathan Lindsay, Cristina Leria (both of FAO), Richard Swinburne and Simon Gleeson (of Richards Butler, International Law Firm) in the preparation of a highly informative legal section (Annex 2 to this report). Thanks are also due to the directors and staff of the following institutions: Quedan and Rural Credit Guarantee Corporation (Quedancor), the Philippines; the Central Warehousing Corporation, India; the Programme pour la Restructuration du Marché Céréalier (PRMC) and the Institut d'Economie Rurale (IER), Mali; TechnoServe (Ghana) Ltd., the Agricultural Development Bank, Barclays Bank (Ghana) Ltd., the Ghana Food Distribution Corporation (GFDC) and the Société Général de Surveillance (SGS) (Ghana) Ltd., Ghana; and the Grain and Feed Trades Association (GAFTA), based in London, United Kingdom.

The authors also thank colleagues who have assisted in the preparation and editing of this publication, including Richard Roberts, Ed Seidler, Pekka Hussi, Anton Slangen, Lawrence Christy, Jaime Novoa, Åke Olofsson (all of FAO), and Paul Hindmarsh, Peter Tyler and Chris Haines (of NRI).

Acronyms

ADB	Agricultural Development Bank, Ghana
BNDA	Agricultural Development Bank, Mali
BULOG	Badan Urusan Logistik, Indonesia
CM-Gs	Commodity Certificates with Guaranteed Delivery
CWC	Central Warehousing Corporation, India
FAO	Food and Agriculture Organization of the United Nations
FAQ	Fair Average Quality
FCI	Food Corporation of India
GAFTA	Grain and Feed Trades Association
GFDC	Ghana Food Distribution Corporation
IER	Institut d'Economie Rurale, Mali
MIS	Market Information Services
NGO	non-governmental organization
NFA	National Food Authority, Philippines
NRI	Natural Resources Institute
ODA	Overseas Development Administration
OPAM	l'Office des Produits Agricoles du Mali
PDS	Public Distribution System, India
PRMC	Programme pour la Restructuration du Marché Céréalier, Mali
Quedancor	Quedan and Rural Credit Guarantee Corporation, Philippines
RBI	Reserve Bank of India
SGS	Société Général de Surveillance (Ghana) Ltd.
WFP	World Food Programme

Summary

This publication addresses a problem which has emerged in recent years in many, if not most, countries which have liberalized their agricultural marketing systems. Such changes are being witnessed in Eastern Europe and states of the former Soviet Union as well as in many developing countries.

Government marketing boards and parastatals usually had ready access to finance to enable them to purchase and to store food and industrial crops. Following liberalization, such finance has not been easily available to private traders who are expected to take over the marketing functions previously carried out by the state. Particularly in the case of food crops, this lack of finance places the burden of storage on farmers who are not always well equipped to store efficiently. The consequence of this is high levels of inter-seasonal price instability, to the detriment of producers and consumers alike.

Inventory credit is one way of overcoming financing constraints. This is not a new concept; archaeological evidence shows that it was practised in Ancient Rome. Obtaining finance against stocks of a wide range of products held in bonded warehouses is common in much of the world. Inventory credit for agricultural produce is widely used in Latin American countries and in some Asian countries (see Case Studies 1 and 2). In many countries, however, it is seldom practised and real estate remains the main form of collateral acceptable to banks.

Various different approaches to inventory credit are presented. For countries discarding interventionist systems or with little experience of commercial storekeeping, an approach is suggested involving a three-cornered arrangement between a bank, a borrower and a warehouse operator. The borrower can be a trader, a miller, a large farmer or a group of farmers. The warehouse operator is generally an organization which is specialized in this field and which does not trade in the produce stored.

Inventory credit is of use in financing the procurement and storage of durable agricultural produce, including: (a) cash crops destined for export markets, (b) imported produce, usually held in bond, for which the importer needs finance during disposal, and (c) domestic food and feed crops, particularly grains, subject to seasonal gluts. This publication is mainly concerned with the last use.

In the case of foodgrain for domestic consumption, inventory credit would involve a borrower negotiating a line of credit, to be made available against the presentation of warehouse receipts. At harvest time, he or she deposits grain at the warehouse as security for a bank loan. This can then be used to purchase further produce, which can itself be pledged as security for a further loan. In this way the borrower's stocks can be increased well beyond his or her initial means. When market prices rise, he or she repays the bank, either in full or in part, pays the warehousing charges and withdraws the relevant quantity of grain for sale on the market. If the borrower does not repay the loan by the due date, the bank seizes the grain and sells it to a third party.

However, in many countries, before this apparently simple commercial transaction can be implemented, various requirements need to be fulfilled. The publication discusses these in detail, with reference to case studies in the Philippines, India, Mali and Ghana. The main conclusion which emerges is that inventory credit should not be "targeted" at particular users, but should be offered without subsidy to those who are able to use it profitably. Similarly, the exercise should be profitable to the lender and the borrower alike, and lending decisions should be made by banks without any kind of external pressure.

Setting up inventory credit as some kind of development "scheme" should be avoided. The banks, rather than Government should be the prime movers, and successful implementation depends above all upon their capabilities. Sustainable results are more likely to be obtained if they provide credit from their own resources, rather than using concessional funds from donors or governments. Outside assistance may, however, be useful to create the appropriate enabling environment for inventory credit to work, e.g. by promoting the concept, by assisting with the drafting of necessary legislation and by supporting the establishment of market information systems.

A crucial element of inventory credit is the availability of reliable warehouse operators. These should not only have the necessary infrastructure and technical skills in storage management and pest control, but should also have business skills and independence from political pressure, which will provide a reasonable guarantee of the integrity of the stocks. A key to getting banks to make a serious commitment to this sort of lending is the presence of warehouse operators of outstanding reputation. For this reason it may be appropriate to involve companies of international repute, or leading national enterprises, in setting up these services. Companies with a background in inspection services, freight- forwarding or pest control may be suitable. In some cases the banks may see fit to set up their own warehousing subsidiaries to carry out a range of collateral management activities concerned with domestic or internationally traded goods.

The establishment of inventory credit in any country requires a careful analysis of the existing legal framework and, on the basis of this, legislative reform may be needed to protect the interests of the parties involved, and to facilitate trading in warehouse receipts.

Inventory credit can only function in a conducive policy environment. It also requires the availability of support services such as market information. Government, will need to accept that traders are entitled to make profits from crop storage. There should be no controls on grain stocking or on the movement of produce, nor any price controls. Government trading, through parastatals and other government-supported bodies should be strictly limited. Policies regarding introduction of food aid onto the market should be transparent and adhered to at all times. Finally, it is likely that inventory credit will not be able to function in countries where there are high or volatile real interest rates.

These conclusions, based on a number of individual experiences, are believed to have a significant degree of general applicability. In particular, they have been corroborated by practical experience in Ghana, where NRI promoted the introduction of a pilot scheme for the financing of the maize trade, and thus was well placed to monitor closely the issues bearing on its utility and viability.

Lastly, it is noted that inventory credit is a significant step in the modernization of agricultural marketing systems. In the longer term, it can facilitate the development of more efficient commodity trading, based on standard grades. Brazilian experience suggests that in some countries it can lead to the creation of commodity-based financial instruments, thereby involving the public at large in the financing of agricultural trade.

Introduction

This publication aims to address a problem which is widespread in developing countries, and others which are liberalizing their agricultural marketing systems, i.e. the lack of finance for trading and inter-seasonal storage of durable agricultural commodities, particularly grain crops. Since the early 1980s in Africa and more recently in E Europe, the problem has been of increasing concern due the general trend away from marketing by state-controlled marketing bodies to marketing by private traders.

In sub-Saharan Africa, the scenario for food commodities is typically as follows. Marketing boards used to enjoy privileged access to bank funds for buying maize or other foodgrains but the private traders, who in most countries now dominate the trade, have only limited access. As a consequence, the trading sector must live on a hand-to-mouth basis, quickly turning over stock in order to avoid running out of funds. Seasonal price variability is often large as there is little cash for buying up stocks to be sold off in the lean season. As a result of these changes to marketing systems, the burden of storage is increasingly being placed on farmers.

Among banks, there is a general reluctance to lend to private traders in domestically produced foods. This seems to be for the following reasons.

(a) Traders are mainly within the informal sector, often keep no written records, have limited resources and have little contact with the banking system.

(b) Lending for agricultural trade involves significant risks, due to the difficulties of accurately forecasting price movements and to deterioration of the produce if improperly stored.

(c) Much of the policy environment surrounding African banks appears to encourage conservatism and discourage the development of new lending instruments. Liquidity controls, imposed as a result of structural adjustment and the high level of interest which banks can obtain on treasury bonds, diminish their interest in finding new private sector clientele. Apart from this, banks often entertain lingering uncertainty about government policies towards private traders in staple commodities, even after markets have been liberalized. In most of the post-independence period, traders have been stigmatized as exploiters, and on occasions have been subject to price controls and even seizures. Bankers may wonder whether the new policies will be rigorously upheld, particularly in times of food crisis.

One of the main limitations on lending for private trade is the requirement for conventional guarantees. In developed countries, stored produce is widely accepted as collateral for lending. For example, in the United Kingdom, banks will typically advance a farmer or trader 80 percent of the market value of grain which is stored in an authorized warehouse and duly insured against losses arising from fire, theft and damage by unusual weather conditions.

In most African countries such financing is seldom available and, if so, only for financing stocks of commodities entering the export or import trade. The main form of collateral acceptable in Africa is real estate, but this greatly limits the feasible volume of lending. Most rural real estate has no market value and is unusable for this purpose. Land is largely untitled. Even in urban areas, traders often have little or no real estate to their name.

Many traders do, however, have some working capital. Stocks purchased by a trader with this capital could be pledged as security for a bank loan, thereby increasing total funds available to him or her for trading.

A solution to the trade financing problem, therefore, could involve increased usage of stocks of commodities as a physical guarantee, an approach which in this paper is referred to as "inventory credit". Indeed this approach may be a key to forging strong long-term links between the banks and the trading sector. It should be noted that banks will not rely exclusively on inventories as collateral, but will tend to use them in combination with more conventional guarantees. By doing this they will be able to increase their total volume of lending to trade customers, and attract new business from informal sector customers who have hitherto been unable to meet all the collateral requirements.

This publication also aims to assist those who are looking for ways of increasing the role and efficiency of private-sector trading, as well as those who simply wish to develop new lending instruments, and is targeted principally at the following types of reader:

- banks, wanting to increase and diversify their clientele through new lending instruments
- companies involved or interested in commercial storekeeping
- traders and farmers who wish to tap new lending sources, as well as the organizations, such as Chambers of Agriculture and Commerce and farmers' associations, which represent them
- policy makers concerned with trade and agriculture, and those influencing the policy-making process
- donors, recognizing the need for trade credit and interested in funding activities necessary to create an enabling environment for inventory credit to function.

The experiences of various countries which have attempted to introduce inventory credit or other trade financing mechanisms are examined through case studies from two Asian (Philippines and India) and two African (Mali and Ghana) countries (see Case Studies 1-5). The case studies refer to cereal crops, but the reader should be aware that inventory credit can work for any durable commodity which exhibits seasonal price variations, including items such as cowpeas, palm oil, dried fish and dried chillies, and commodities entering international trade. The successful introduction of inventory credit for food crops may, in turn, open opportunities for the concept to be extended to other commodities.

Section 1

Why it is important to improve trade financing

The situation described below, encountered in a survey of 357 wholesale grain traders in Tanzania, has features in common with many African countries. While this fragmented trade structure encourages competition, it is far from ideal. Traders are generally under-capitalized, and seldom engage in inter-seasonal storage to take advantage of seasonal price rises. They prefer to turn over their stock quickly and obtain a modest, but assured, profit.

WHOLESALE GRAIN TRADERS IN TANZANIA, LATE 1991

The traders' scales of operation were typically small. At the time of interview, 58 percent of maize traders and 71 percent of rice traders handled 25 bags or less per shipment. For traders moving grain between locations, the average number of bags handled was 37 for maize and 25 for rice, with three shipments normally being made per month.

There were few links in the market chain between producer and consumer, and three-quarters of the traders claimed to have bought directly from farmers. They had developed little specialization in their functions.

Few traders had any trucks and they usually had to rely on hired transport, which was often difficult to find. They generally lacked storage facilities in the towns, and bags of grain were mainly kept in the open, giving rise to storage problems.

Only 2 percent of traders used bank credit, almost entirely larger traders dealing in rice, and their access was very restricted by lack of money on the banks' side. The three most important problems identified were credit (49 percent), transport (49 percent) and storage (31 percent).

Source: Marketing Development Bureau, Dar es Salaam (1992)

With a decline in the level of public-sector stockholding, and little storage on the part of traders, farmers find themselves obliged to hold on to stocks which in previous years would have been purchased by the parastatals. In African countries, such stocks are held in rustic storage cribs or granaries made from locally available materials, including wood, mud and various thatching materials.

In general terms, increased on-farm storage is a desirable outcome of liberalization, relieving the State of much of the costs of holding commercial food stocks, and making an important contribution to local and national food security. Given the low level of investment required, it is often the cheapest form of storage. Unfortunately, farmers often experience problems in storing large quantities of grain. Notwithstanding the prospect of higher lean-season prices, they are often forced to sell grain either to satisfy immediate cash needs or to avoid storage problems. Such problems are particularly acute where farmers grow hybrid varieties of maize – due to their susceptibility to pests – and in areas where rainfall occurs after harvesting. In some countries, farmers grow traditional varieties of maize for home consumption during the year, while hybrid varieties are cultivated for the market. Traditional storage techniques are usually adequate for storing the traditional varieties but not for hybrids, which must be disposed of quickly in order to avoid spoilage.

These constraints suggest that farmers should not be relied upon exclusively to carry out the inter-seasonal stocking function within liberalized marketing systems. In the absence of commercial storage, there is likely to be a high degree of price variability between harvest time and the lean season.

Empirical evidence from Africa (see Annex 1) shows that the degree of inter-seasonal price variability is often high, and is also extremely variable from country to country, and from crop to crop. Available data indicate that the average increase in lean-season over harvest prices ranges from around 31 percent in Sahelian countries to over 100 percent in Ghana.

The main determinant of price variability is the speed at which farmers release grain onto the market, and the amount they hold back as precautionary reserves. In Ghana, maize is predominantly a cash crop in the main surplus-producing areas, and for this reason farmers do not hold precautionary reserves. Moreover, on-farm storage is made difficult by high humidity at the time of harvest and, until very recently, private traders have made little use of mechanical dryers. By contrast, farmers in Sahelian countries often hold stocks of millet and sorghum for several years. Grain is usually dry at harvest time and, stored on the sheath, losses are minimal. Farmers have a much greater role in buffering inter-seasonal price fluctuations than in the case with maize in Ghana and neighbouring coastal states.

In many African countries the level of inter-seasonal price variability is likely to increase during the 1990s due to the effect of market liberalization. This is particularly true of countries like Malawi, Zimbabwe, Kenya and Zambia which had been relatively effective in enforcing their public sector grain monopolies.

Another problem noted in the study of the Tanzanian marketing system is considerable short-term price fluctuation (Marketing Development Bureau, 1992), due to the absence of intermediate-level stockholding between the farmer and the consumer. In Dar es Salaam, feed millers were unable to find wholesale merchants who could supply stocks of grain on demand, but were dependent upon a flow of trucks arriving from distant supplying locations (Coulter and Golob, 1992).

Price instability of the kinds described and associated low levels of commercial stockholding are believed to be disadvantageous to society for the following reasons.

- Farmers receive lower prices in the immediate post-harvest period, when they often need to sell to satisfy cash needs and to repay production loans. This leads to lower use of purchased inputs and mechanization services and, hence, to lower overall output.

- Consumers in urban areas, who typically spend a large proportion of their household budget on staple foods, are required to adjust their expenditure in the light of changing prices for food staples.

- The absence of intermediate stocks between farmer and consumer, or user, increases the level of post-harvest losses. This appears to be the case in Ghana, where it has been calculated that farmers lose between 6 and 8 percent of their maize crop over storage periods of between three and seven months (Ofusu, quoted by Boxall and Bickersteth, 1991[1]). With well-managed commercial storage, however, losses can be reduced to 2 percent or less over an eight-month period[2]. However, achieving this in tropical climates is not a simple matter; a high level of technical and managerial competence is required.

- Also, the absence of intermediate stocks discourages trade between regions and countries, and diminishes the use of local cereals *vis-à-vis* imports and food aid. The consequent lower demand for locally produced grains has an adverse effect on production and employment in the rural economy. One of the most notable cases is that of feed-maize in Ghana. This country has been shown to have a comparative advantage in producing maize for domestic consumption (World Bank, 1991), but credit terms vastly favour imports, with the United States Government underwriting three-month revolving lines of credit for US yellow maize.

For these reasons the authors believe that there is a strong case for improving the financing of agricultural trade in Africa. In some countries (e.g. Ghana), the high degree of price variability suggests that traders will wish to use inventory credit in almost every year. In other cases, as with millet and sorghum in Sahelian countries, traders are likely to use inventory credit services on a more opportunistic basis, when they are trying to accumulate stocks for export to neighbouring countries, or when they judge that market prices may increase substantially, as happened in 1988 and late 1990 (see Annex 1, Figure A2).

Better trade financing should result in a higher degree of inter-temporal market integration. Over the long term, this will happen as follows. As closer links are forged between the financial and commercial sectors, funds will increasingly flow backwards and forwards between them. As already happens in developed countries and some of the more advanced economies in the developing world, trade will attract commodity finance seeking

---

[1] While estimation of on-farm storage losses is subject to wide margins of error, NRI grain storage experts consider Ofusu's figures to be of the correct order of magnitude.

[2] There is also considerable scope for reducing on-farm storage losses through better handling and pest control. For this reason increased storage in commercial warehouses should be seen simply as complementing improved storage by farmers.

speculative profit. Indeed finance will continue to be attracted up to the point of what economists call "normal profits", i.e. the minimum level of profit to attract those who are speculating on price rises.

Indonesian experience suggests how better trade financing can reduce inter-seasonal price variability: during the 1980s average spreads were only 11 percent (Trotter, 1992). This low level can be attributed to several causes, including lower production variability than is the norm in Africa, and the intervention of the parastatal, Badan Urusan Logistik (BULOG). However, much of the smoothing can be attributed to the fact that millers have adequate access to finance to cover their stockholding needs.

Section 2

How can inventory credit be implemented?

Bankers' willingness to lend depends upon their being confident that the loan will be well used and repaid. With inventory credit, they need to be reassured that their physical collateral is totally secure, that its physical integrity will be preserved and that it will not be misappropriated under any circumstances.

ALTERNATIVE APPROACHES

Several alternative approaches to implementation have been identified:

(a) centralized warehouses or silos managed by a specialized warehouse operator[3], which does not trade in the items stored, but simply holds the stock as security for bank lending;

(b) centralized warehouses or silos operated by a specialized warehouse operator, which also acts as a channel for bank lending to a number of individual borrowers (alternatively, banks could operate warehouses directly or through subsidiary companies);

(c) centralized warehouses managed by a storekeeper, who is also a trader;

(d) warehouses operated by individual borrowers, under the supervision of a surveillance company;

(e) warehouses operated jointly by the borrower(s) and a bank under a dual-key arrangement.

The limited experience to date suggests that in countries which are establishing inventory credit arrangements for the first time, approach (a) is likely to

---

[3]"Warehouse operators" may also be referred to as "storekeepers" or "collateral managers" - the latter in the case where the company concerned is holding produce in trust for a bank.

have the best prospects. Its principal advantages are the high degree of security it gives lenders, by assuring that the warehouse operator is independent of the borrower, its contribution to the transparency of the trading system, and the fact that it avoids the administrative complications of a dual-key arrangement in (e).

Approach (c) is widely practised by larger trading companies in Europe and North America. Storekeepers offer farmers the choice of either storing their crop or buying it from them, though when storage is in short supply, they may only offer to buy, as this allows the storekeeper greater profit. Such arrangements are likely to evolve as countries become more developed. In Brazil, the warehousing law was recently amended to allow warehouse operators to trade on their own account.

In countries which have little experience in commercial storekeeping and no effective law for the regulation of warehousing practice, banks are likely to prefer approach (a). This is because it eliminates risks that the warehouse operator will be bankrupted by trading activities, and thereby risk the viability of the entire lending operation.

Approach (d) may be attractive in cases where warehouses are too small for a storekeeper to operate economically. In other cases, a single borrower may buy so much produce that he or she can fill a single store. In these circumstances, the bank may be content for the borrower to hold the stocks, providing that they are regularly inspected by a surveillance company. If the borrower disposes of the grain without the bank's authorization, the bank can bring criminal charges. This is the approach adopted successfully in the Philippines (Case Study 1).

In approach (a), bankers' confidence in the integrity of the collateral is assured by a highly professional warehouse operator, but in the Philippines this is done in another way: a government-owned corporation underwrites the banks' lending. Moreover, the parastatal grain trading organization undertakes to buy up any unsold stock at an official floor price.

The first approach is discussed in greater detail, as this is seen as the most viable approach in countries with little experience of inventory credit. The Philippine model has interesting features, but may be inappropriate in countries trying to rid themselves of interventionist policies, since the creation of official guarantee funds and floor prices creates opportunities both for special interest lobbying and abuse of state power. One characteristic of the scheme is that it is supported by an interest-rate subsidy. Due to this subsidy, it is not known whether the scheme increases millers' propensity to store, or whether it simply finances storage which, in its absence, would be financed in other ways.

MECHANICS OF INVENTORY CREDIT

There are three essential parties (see Figure 1) to a commercial inventory credit scheme of scheme type (a).

- The borrower, who uses the produce as a security for a loan.
- The lender, usually a bank, which is looking for a relatively secure way to lend its funds and expand its clientele.
- The warehouse operator, a third party, which maintains the produce in good condition and assures the lender that the collateral is secure. The warehouse operator will hold the grain in a warehouse or, possibly, silo

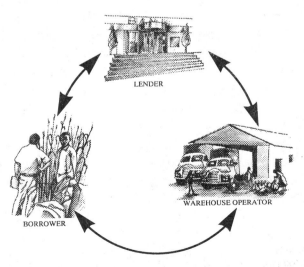

FIGURE 1
Essential parties in inventory credit

that it either owns or leases from another party. The borrower is charged fees to cover the cost of warehouse rent, managing the grain and insuring it against fire and unusual weather conditions. The qualities required to perform successfully as a warehouse operator are discussed in Section 4. The procedure for lending, storing and repayment works as follows (it is assumed that the produce stored is grain).

(a) Well in advance of the harvest, the borrower applies for credit facilities to be made available against presentation of warehouse receipts.

(b) The bank approves (or rejects) the application, based upon the criteria it has developed for this kind of lending. It will probably fix a "cash credit limit" up to which it will lend for the next season. At this time a tripartite agreement may be drawn up between the bank, the borrower and the warehouse operator (see Annex 3).

(c) At harvest time the borrower has grain which he or she has bought or, in the case of larger farmers, was produced by the farmer. After drying and cleaning the grain, he or she takes it to the warehouse.

(d) The warehouse operator checks that the grain meets minimum quality standards which have been established for content of moisture, foreign matter, live insects, etc. If it meets the standards, it is accepted for storage and the borrower is given a warehouse receipt showing the number of bags, the weight and the quality of the produce received (see Annex 4).

(e) The borrower presents the receipt to the bank as security for a loan. As approval has already been given up to the cash credit limit, the loan is made immediately. This avoids time-consuming procedures whenever the trader deposits grain in the store. The bank makes the loan based on the current market valuation of the grain. Usually, it will lend up to a given percentage of the value of the grain deposited, e.g. 80 percent, requiring the borrower to finance the "margin" of 20 percent from his own resources[4]. The term of the loan will be related to the annual price

---

[4]The margin is likely to vary according to the banks' assessment of the risk and the extent of any other collateral which the depositor is able to provide. The figure of 80 percent is frequently quoted as giving adequate protection to the bank while providing sufficient incentive to the trader to undertake inventory credit.

pattern; the borrower is required to repay before the time when prices normally pass their seasonal peak.

(f) The borrower may now use the loan proceeds to purchase more grain either for trading or for further deposit in the warehouse. The warehouse receipts may be used as security for further loans, and so on. In this way a borrower may greatly increase his or her funds invested in grain stocks. Take, for example, a trader who starts with an initial stock of 100 tonnes of grain purchased with his own funds. After pledging three times, he or she may have bought three times as much grain as he or she would have purchased without access to inventory credit:

Impact of inventory credit on stockholding
Quantity purchased with loan of 80 percent (tonnes):

Initial stock	100
Purchase with first loan	80
Purchase with second loan	64
Purchase with third loan	51
TOTAL	295

The total shown only applies when the procurement price remains stable throughout the purchasing period. Since it generally rises, the borrower will, with each loan, be able to buy less grain than the amount shown. If this happens, it may be justified for the lender to revalue the entire stock in store, and recalculate the borrower's entitlement accordingly.

(g) Grain belonging to individual borrowers may either be stored separately from that of other borrowers (i.e. "identity is preserved"), or mixed with grain belonging to other borrowers ("identity is confused"). In the latter case, the grain which the warehouse operator finally issues is of a standard quality, but is unlikely to be the same lot which was originally deposited in the warehouse. The pros and cons of preserving identity are set out on page 16.

(h) The borrower withdraws the grain when he or she wishes to sell it, probably in the lean season, either in one lot or in separate tranches. To withdraw grain the borrower must first settle his or her bills with the

PROS AND CONS OF PRESERVING THE IDENTITY OF PRODUCE

The advantage of confusing the identity of produce is that it allows for economical use of grain cleaning and drying equipment, and of storage space, and makes for faster movement in and out of store. For this reason, the warehouse operator in the Ghanaian case study, which has a network of silo sites with grain dryers and cleaners, is following the policy of confusing identity (see Case Study 4). In situations where warehouse operators have large dryers (e.g. requiring a minimum batch of 20 tonnes), they may have little choice but to confuse identity. Most depositor borrowers are unable to fill the capacity of the dryer on each occasion it is used: some mixing inevitably occurs. Similar considerations apply to the use of large silos.

Warehouse operators which have drying and cleaning equipment are able to bring heterogeneous lots down to a uniform quality standard. Based on a knowledge of initial and final moisture content and the quantity of foreign matter and damaged grain removed, the warehouse operator can tell each depositor borrower how much grain he or she should receive upon issue.

An advantage of preserving identity is that it helps develop trust between the depositor borrower and the warehouse operator. As in the case in India (Case Study 2) the depositor borrower knows that he or she will get back the same grain he or she deposited, and will not be subsidizing others who deliver produce of poor quality. A further advantage of preserving identity is that it allows warehouse operators to operate more flexible quality standards and grading criteria. Grain is stored providing it is sufficiently dry and meets a minimum standard for foreign matter, etc., but it need not meet a uniform trade standard. Traders will sometimes prefer this arrangement, as it means they can minimize loss of weight through grain cleaning.

Preserving identity is, therefore, likely to prove most attractive in situations where traders are unsophisticated and reluctant to trust their grain to safekeeping by others; in drier climates where grain does not need mechanical drying prior to storage; and where there is an abundance of inexpensive warehouse storage, permitting storage of small, discreet lots without jeopardizing the profitability of the warehouse operator.

warehouse operator and repay the bank with accumulated interest and bank charges. However, in practice, the bank may allow its good customers to obtain release of the grain before repaying the loan.

(i) In the event that borrowers fail to repay the loan fully by the due date, the bank will be authorized to seize and auction the grain. If proceeds are not adequate to cover the full amount, the bank should follow its normal procedures for recovering overdue debts.

Section 3

Key requirements for successful implementation

Seven key requirements for the successful implementation of inventory credit are outlined here.

❑ **Inventory credit should be perceived as potentially profitable by all parties involved, and should not be viewed as a public service function**

For many readers, this observation may seem obvious. However, it is a principle which can often be overlooked where governments and development assistance programmes are concerned, as illustrated by the schemes implemented for traders in Mali (Case Study 3). In this case it appears that the banks and one of the storekeepers saw inventory credit more as a public service function to be carried out on behalf of Government or donors, rather than as a long-term business venture to which they themselves were committed.

Those wishing to promote the development of inventory credit should seek out banks which are financially sound, have adequate resources for lending, are interested in expanding their clientele, have a record of innovation, and are known for their speed of operation and their willingness to adapt loan conditions to changes in the condition and pattern of trade. It should not be assumed that "agricultural banks" or "rural banks" are suitable. Notwithstanding their mandate, they often fail to fulfil these essential criteria.

There should be no political pressure to lend and, generally speaking, special lines of credit or specific central bank rediscounting facilities should be avoided. There may be a special case for the latter when there is a severe seasonal credit shortage.

In line with this thinking, warehouse operators should not be required to carry out costly social roles on behalf of Government, for example, to receive uneconomically small lots of produce. Situations where warehouse operators required minimum amounts of produce to operate their dryers economically (e.g. 20 tonnes) are referred to on page 16. Even where dryers are not needed, warehouse operators will always need to establish minimum lot sizes, since handling, weighing, quality control and administrative costs are all high when receiving a few bags at a time. Preserving identity of small individual lots will also make for high storage costs. Likewise banks will incur high costs when processing very small disbursements. For these reasons, the best way of providing inventory credit to small farmers or small traders is by encouraging them to associate into informal groups or co-operatives, and thereby bulk-up volumes which are economical for the warehouse operator to handle.

The concern for profitability also means that inventory credit should not be exclusively for a single commodity, e.g. maize, but should be open to any commodity for which traders need to obtain finance against their stockholding. The range of commodities stored by traders is likely to include items such as coarse grains, rice, fertilizer, seed, cement, sugar, tea, cocoa, coffee, dried fish and grain bags. A caveat must, however, be added for those cases where equipment, physiological or phytosanitary problems limit the range of products which can be stored together.

☐ Borrowers must put up equity alongside their credit

An important aspect of inventory lending is that the borrower has some initial equity in the form of grain which he or she has bought or, in the case of the farmer, has produced. This stock is deposited as collateral for credit. As noted earlier, lending will usually be for less than the market value of the grain, so that a borrower continues to have some equity tied up in the stock.

☐ Appropriate lending rules and speed of operation

For the borrower, this is the most important requirement. It is vital to avoid unnecessary red tape and guarantees which slow down the lending process without a commensurate increase in security. Funds should be disbursed to borrowers immediately upon presentation of warehouse receipts.

Traditional bank evaluation procedures can be followed at the time the trader initially applies for a line of credit. Subsequently, however, loan disbursement and repayment procedures must be more or less immediate in order to permit the trader to take advantage of profitable trading opportunities. Moreover, branch managers should have certain discretionary limits up to which they may release funds to customers without reference to higher authority.

A problem noted in the Ghanaian case study (Case Study 4) is that banks which are unfamiliar with inventory credit tend to apply ground rules developed for other forms of lending, which are inappropriate for this type of trading where speedy decision-making is of the essence. This is particularly the case when borrowers are asked to put up real estate as collateral, in addition to inventory.

It is understandable that banks seek this additional security from borrowers who can provide it, but valuations and searches tend to be extremely time-consuming. Insistence upon real estate as security shortly before the onset of a harvest may cause the borrower to lose the opportunity to buy produce when prices are lowest. Instead of enhancing the security of the loan, the mechanical application of standard rules reduces the profitability of the borrower's operation, and thereby diminishes the bank's security.

The same is true of rules requiring borrowers to have a full set of accounts and to present projected cash flow statements for the period of the loan. Many of the most capable grain traders are in the informal sector and do not keep detailed accounts. Some may be illiterate. This is not to say that they should not be encouraged to keep records, but the inflexible application of such ground rules may bias lending in favour of more educated borrowers lacking the necessary experience to operate successfully as traders. This again renders lending less rather than more secure.

The most important criterion for inventory lending should be the borrower's professionalism and track record in the business concerned. Any reputation and credit history that the borrower may have should also be taken into consideration. Thus, references should be given far more weight than the provision of real estate or keeping of elaborate formal accounts, although some form of record will be required in order to establish the maximum level of credit which should be extended.

Ultimately, bank lending is about managing risk: how banks can approach this task in the case of inventory lending is discussed in Section 6.

□ Reliable and reputable warehouse operators

It is not important for the warehouse operator to be a store owner; the operator may simply lease the warehouses or silos. It is preferable if the operator has the possession of, or access to, equipment for drying and cleaning produce, but even this is not essential. The warehouse operator can insist that produce brought to its store is dry and meets certain standards of cleanliness.

As regards efficiency and reliability, however, there should be no compromise. If the warehouse operator cannot ensure the physical security of the collateral, the banks will decline to lend. Failure in this regard was one of the main problems with the Malian trader schemes.

Good warehouse operators are most likely to be found if banks are responsible for their selection, since it is the banks which stand to lose most in the event of a poor decision. The following criteria are suggested for assessing suitability:

(a) access to suitably located storage facilities and, where needed, equipment for drying and cleaning produce;

(b) staff technically competent in grain handling and storage, including grading, quality control and fumigation;

(c) a good track record in the warehousing business;

(d) financial resources and reputation, as a guarantee that restitution will be made in the case of unsatisfactory performance of duties - the bank may alternatively seek a performance bond;

(e) business skills, involving the speedy and efficient management of warehousing and warranting services, and good communications with customers and banks;

(f) an entrepreneurial outlook and ability to innovate - in order that inventory credit be made widely available, a warehouse operator will need to sell its services actively in different parts of the country where there are marketable crop surpluses, and among those seeking to use it in relation to international trade;

(g) motivated and, by implication, well-paid staff;

(h) the ability to withstand political pressure, such as pressure from a Government faced with a food emergency and seeking to requisition food stocks - for this reason, it may be preferable in some countries that warehouse operators be private sector organizations, or even multinational companies (see also Sections 6 and 7).

It is possible for existing parastatal grain trading companies to become warehouse operators, but there are various problems associated with this option (see Section 7). Finding suitable private warehouse operators may also be difficult in some countries. Companies interested in warehousing may lack an adequate track record and/or net worth to satisfy the banks' requirements. There is also a danger of conflict-of-interest where prospective warehouse operators are reluctant to separate warehousing from trading activities, as required by the preferred approach (a) described in Section 2.

In the absence of reputable warehouse operators, it may be best to involve companies which perform related services such as freight-forwarding, inspection and pest control. Such companies may operate warehouses as an adjunct to their core business and have access to the necessary skills. An alternative is for the banks to set up their own storekeeping subsidiaries, either individually, or with several banks acting in concert.

In some countries, the key to successful collateral management may be to involve major blue-chip companies, either multinationals or large national concerns, whose participation is seen by the banks as an assurance that any failure on the part of the warehouse operator will be made good. While multinationals are not immune from corruption, any more than smaller local companies and parastatals, they are likely to avoid any gross mismanagement or contractual failure that would damage their international business standing.

The blue-chip company will preferably, but not necessarily, be one with experience in the warehousing of agricultural commodities. It may operate as a storekeeper in its own right, or associate with a smaller local company with relevant skills. An example of such an association is that of a pest control company in Mali, which recently joined forces with a leading multinational superintendent company to inspect rice stocks pledged as security by a parastatal rice miller.

◻ Availability of market intelligence

Market intelligence is essential for both lenders and borrowers in order to minimize the speculative risks involved in storing agricultural produce. In Africa, most governments have Early Warning Units producing crop forecasts, while some have Market Information Services (MIS) which disseminate price and other information.

These organizations provide valuable information but are usually under-funded. Generally, they have been initiated through donor programmes but attempts to incorporate them as part of ongoing programmes, without outside assistance, are often unsuccessful. They need strengthening and the range of information disseminated needs expanding to include items such as crop forecasts, prices in neighbouring countries, prospective imports and food aid arrivals. Sustainability can often be improved by reducing the number of crops, for which market information is collected, and the number of markets sampled. In setting up market information services there is often a temptation to try to maximize the amount of information collected without regard to its usefulness, or the cost of collection or processing[5].

Dissemination mechanisms generally need improving to ensure that traders and banks have ready access to the information. Radio stations, for example, are often unwilling to broadcast market information without payment of fees which government MIS can ill afford. One option may be to arrange for sponsorship of market information broadcasts. Banks can use this information as well as data from branch networks and informal trade comment. They should have the capability of collating these sources of

---

[5] A new FAO software programme, FAO-Agrimarket, greatly facilitates data processing for MIS.

information in order to assess lending risks. By correlating production and price data, and analysing historical data, they can better forecast price movements.

Creating an analysis capability for a range of agricultural commodities may incur significant costs, and for this reason one possibility might be to centralize such services in an inter-bank organization created for this purpose.

☐ **Appropriate warehousing and commercial legislation**

The establishment of an inventory credit programme requires a careful analysis of the existing legal framework. Among other things, this will entail a review of laws and procedures relating to the sale of goods, secured transactions, and warehouse, banking and credit regulation. The main issues (discussed at greater length in Annex 2) are likely to be as follows.

- The level of protection which laws give a lender *vi-à-vis* third parties who, without knowledge of the lender's interest, buy the produce, or acquire some other kind of interest (such as a security interest) in it. In this regard, it is important to know if the laws provide a tool with which a bank can "perfect" its interest – in other words, a way of giving notice to the world at large of the bank's interest that protects the bank against later claimants. In many countries, a system of registering charges provides this protection.
- The level of protection which laws give a lender in the event of the death or bankrupcy of the borrower or the warehouse operator.
- Whether the laws recognize warehouse receipts as negotiable documents of title. This will greatly increase the attractiveness of warehouse receipts to lenders as security for loans.
- Whether stored produce can be "pledged" to secure a loan. In many countries pledging may give the lender adequate security even where it is not possible to register charges.
- Whether lenders can obtain an effective security with goods which are mixed as part of an undifferentiated bulk.
- Whether the legal personality of the borrower has an effect on the lender's security.

There is considerable variation between countries in the amount of legislation on this topic. Civil Law (or Code Law) countries, including countries of Latin America and Francophone Africa, and those whose legal systems stem from the model of post-revolutionary France, tend to have a considerable amount of legislation. In Common Law countries, there is more reliance on customary practice. Nethertheless, three important Common Law countries, the United States, the Philippines (see Case Study 1) and India (Case Study 2) have comprehensive statutory frameworks.

It is stressed that the "practical" effects of a particular legal variable on the viability of inventory credit will usually not be evident from an examination of legal doctrine alone. Where the economics of the scheme are strong enough, and lenders are comfortable that the practical risks are small, they may be able to live with a certain amount of legal ambiguity. Where, however, the economics are unclear and the political and business culture is unaccustomed to what is being proposed, legal uncertainties may present another reason for sceptical participants, particularly banks, to turn away from an uncertain venture. Thus, the establishment of inventory credit may require some persuasive and creative contribution from lawyers or, in the final analysis, legislative reform.

Legal frameworks may be strong on paper but weak in practice. This is particularly true of legal provisions which specify the duties and responsibilities of warehouse operators, notable features of Philippine and Indian legislation. In some countries these provisions may provide real protection to a bank when dealing with a relatively unknown operator. In other countries, the bank's only protection is its knowledge of the operator, particularly regarding its competence, reputation and financial resources.

❐ Negotiability of warehouse receipts

Even if legislation is not needed to establish inventory credit, it may be needed to convert receipts into negotiable documents of title. In the UK these are known as "bearer warrants".

Negotiability brings major advantages (an extensive discussion can be found in Annex 2). Upon receiving a negotiable warehouse receipt, the holder is entitled to the goods described in it, whatever the depositor or the warehouse operator has done to them in the meantime. Negotiability allows goods to be traded freely on the market by specification, i.e. without visual inspection of the commodity concerned. Produce is sold simply by endorsing the receipt in favour of the buyer. This helps reduce transaction costs and facilitates the development of "forward" and "futures transactions" (see Section 9). If a contract specifies delivery at a certain date in the future, delivery can be carried out simply by the exchange of the receipt.

Negotiability requires the commodity concerned to be specified in terms of standard grades so that the produce can be sold without being seen. For commodities like maize, standard grades can be established by mutual agreement between the warehouse operators and the trade. Grading is further discussed in Section 8.

As indicated above, negotiability can greatly increase the attractiveness to lenders of using warehouse receipts as security. In the event of default by the borrower, the lender can simply sell the warrant to liquidate the collateral, instead of first having to take physical possession of the grain. Negotiability is also a precondition for the emergence of a secondary market in the debt, and gives the lender greater flexibility with respect to its loan portfolio.

Negotiability will depend upon the market's confidence in the warehouse operators that issue the warrants. Confidence can be adversely affected by fear of malpractice or negligence (e.g. not insuring the produce stored) and, with newer warehouse operators, lack of an established reputation in the field. This observation serves to re-emphasize the importance of reliable and reputable warehouse operators.

Section 4
The need for an appropriate political and economic environment

Inventory credit is unlikely to be successful in countries where the macro-economic and policy environment is unsupportive of private trade. Traders will not undertake storage, even for a few months, if they sense a danger that Government will impose price controls, seize stocks (on the ground that traders are "hoarding"), ban exports, permit unscheduled food aid imports and/or suddenly release food security reserve stocks in response to only modest price rises.

The Indian case study (Case Study 2) provides an example of potentially viable inventory credit arrangements, through the use of warehouse deposits, which work imperfectly because both the rice and wheat market and the financial system are heavily regulated by Federal and State Governments. Funds made available to the trading sector are controlled, the percentage of the value of the stored crop against which loans can be obtained is dictated by the Central Bank, and the level of stock which can be held by private traders and millers is also controlled.

In Africa and Eastern Europe, the temptation for governments to adopt a similar approach and try to control the grain market, even after liberalization has supposedly taken place, will remain strong. Policy changes will not remove the residual mistrust of the private sector. Moreover, the provision of inventory credit may actually assist the private trade to "speculate" and this, despite its obvious advantages, may be difficult, politically, for governments to accept.

To introduce inventory credit successfully into a country, the following conditions will need to be satisfied:

- acceptance by the Government that traders are entitled to profits they may earn from storing produce
- absence of any sort of controls on the price, internal movement and private stocks of grain
- limited Government involvement in trading, whether through parastatals or quasi-governmental "co-operatives"
- consistent and transparent policies towards food aid and international trade
- a competent and financially solvent banking sector, free from regulations governing interest rates, the amount which can be lent for inventory credit or the percentage of the value of stock which can be accepted as collateral, and without political interference in management or lending decisions
- moderate and fairly predictable real interest rates.

With regard to government trading, some governments use Food Security Reserves to prevent famine conditions or extreme price fluctuations[6]. It is recommended that government interventions be kept as small as possible consistent with this objective. Where possible, prices should be stabilized by opening up the market to international or intra-regional trade. The problem with large reserves is that government operations are invariably subsidized in one way or another and, if reserves are operated at high levels, they tend to crowd out private operators who have to pay the full costs of storage.

Similar considerations apply to food aid, particularly when the food concerned competes directly with national production. The frequently disruptive effect of food aid on production and marketing incentives is widely documented. Such food aid should be incorporated into Food Security Reserves or, in their absence, be released onto the market in a way which avoids disruption and is based on clear guidelines established in advance of each harvest.

In Africa, only a minority of countries appear to be ready for inventory credit, due to policy frameworks which remain either interventionist or

---

[6]The use of these reserves in African countries is discussed by Coulter (1994).

ambiguous. However, with the implementation of structural adjustment, the situation is constantly changing, and the number of eligible countries is tending to increase slowly.

Free-market reform is a necessary but not a sufficient condition for introducing inventory credit. This is illustrated by the case of Zambia, which has liberalized grain trading, but where the implementation of structural adjustment resulted in erratic and often extremely high real interest rates (reaching well in excess of 100 percent in 1993). Under these circumstances traders were unlikely to borrow for grain storage, fearing that price rises would not compensate for high and unpredictable financing costs.

A further factor which will make it easier to implement inventory credit schemes is the liberalization of trade between adjacent countries. Notwithstanding the arbitrary nature of borders inherited from colonial regimes, African governments have generally adopted highly restrictive policies towards private grain exports. Concerns over domestic food security are normally used to justify restrictions, but this takes little account of the role of intra-regional trade in stabilizing food prices. Moreover, such policies discourage exports at times of grain surplus and reduce the incentive to hold stocks for sale in neighbouring countries.

There is probably no country where at some time market intermediaries have not been held up as unscrupulous exploiters of the people. Terms like *coyote* in Central America or *walangusi* in Tanzania sum up perennial public suspicion about their role. Hard-pressed governments often use traders as scapegoats for hardships experienced by farmers and consumers. Small- or medium-scale traders usually lack powerful political connections, and are an easy target, allowing governments to ignore what are often more fundamental causes, such as lack of employment opportunities in urban areas, thin markets characterized by weak demand and poor policies.

NRI chose Ghana as the most suitable country in Africa in which to promote inventory credit financing on a pilot scale. There were no restrictions on internal trade, and the country had a deregulated banking system and moderate real rates of interest. However, even there, some elements of the policy and institutional framework were unfavourable. For example, a large public sector deficit makes it easy for banks to make money by investing in treasury bills, rather than by searching for new borrowers. Moreover, a lack of definition of the role of the grain marketing parastatal left some ambiguity about the "rules of the game" in which the private sector was expected to operate.

In conclusion, the development of efficient trade financing will be a slow process in many areas of the world. However, facilitation measures as described elsewhere in this paper will undoubtedly assist. Inventory credit should be introduced only in countries where the policy and institutional frameworks are relatively favourable, such that imitation is encouraged through the "demonstration effect".

Section 5

Who can benefit from inventory credit?

SHOULD MILLERS BE FAVOURED?

The pattern of grain marketing varies from country to country and according to the grain concerned. In many developing countries farmers have a leading role in the storage of grain, which they release at intervals during the months following the harvest. Those experiencing storage problems and severe cash constraints will tend to release their crop earlier, giving rise to pronounced seasonal gluts.

The role of millers varies greatly, however, according to whether the mills are of the large commercial kind or small custom-mills. Large commercial mills are typical in many Asian countries, e.g. India, Pakistan, Philippines and Indonesia, where millers tend to move quickly into the business of inter-seasonal storage – providing that government policies are conducive – in order to ensure the availability of operational stocks on a year-round basis. Millers seem to be highly suitable targets for inventory credit in countries where most grain reaches the consumer after commercial milling. One of the largest inventory credit programmes in the developing world is targeted at rice millers in the Philippines (see Case Study 1).

By way of contrast, in most countries in sub-Saharan Africa, grain is normally milled either by pounding in the home or by small custom-mills. Most inter-seasonal storage is carried out on the farm, while traders seek a rapid turnover of stock. In these countries, there appears to be the greatest need for new sources of credit for grain storage by traders although, in time, some custom-mill owners are likely to progress to stockholding.

Some African countries have large commercial milling sectors but these have generally grown up as part of state-controlled marketing systems which took care of all their procurement. With market liberalization, these mills have quickly lost market share to small custom-mills which have lower overheads and are more favourably located *vis-à-vis* producers and consumers. This pattern has been repeated with maize in Kenya, Tanzania, Zimbabwe and Zambia, and in Mali with rice, among other countries. In Africa, therefore, it is unlikely that the large-scale commercial milling sector will quickly move into the storage role along Asian lines.

FARMERS OR TRADERS?

A concern often raised about inventory credit is that it should be directed at the farmer, and not the trader or the middleman, whose role is seen as potentially exploitative.

Several Asian countries, including Thailand and India, operate marketing credit schemes where individual farmers are funded to store grain on their own farms; the schemes are usually tied in with production credit programmes. However, unless there is a subsidy, the cost of lending to individual small farmers tends to be prohibitive, and these schemes have involved heavily subsidizing both supervision costs and interest rates. On account of this, it is difficult to make any general recommendation in favour of marketing credit schemes for farmers. They are particularly difficult to implement in countries with weak rural credit systems, characterized by a dearth of financial institutions and low repayment rates.

Costs of storage by farmers can be reduced to economic levels if they form co-operatives and store collectively. However, the problem with co-operatives is that they tend to develop slowly and to be unsustainable without continued outside support and supervision. In the worst cases, co-operatives are promoted for political reasons and are seen simply as a way of obtaining credit which does not have to be repaid. This was the case with Village Associations in certain parts of Mali (Case Study 3).

Even where co-operatives and similar organizations have been promoted in a more professional manner, questions may be raised about their long-term sustainability. In other parts of Mali, the repayment performance of Village Associations has been good but this is largely attributable to high levels of outside supervision.

Co-operatives engaged in inventory credit under the auspices of the NGO TechnoServe in Ghana (Case Study 5) have experienced considerable financial success. However, despite the organization's continued emphasis on self-reliance, the co-operatives are, as in the Malian case above, highly dependent upon outside supervision. TechnoServe's experience also suggests that success is more likely in high-potential areas or with high-value produce.

The main conclusion which emerges is that, as a general rule, marketing credit should not be targeted exclusively at particular users but should be promoted without subsidy to allcomers, as a business activity which is profitable to both the lender and the borrower, and where lending decisions are made by banks without any kind of external pressure. In most African countries, grain traders are likely to be leading users of such credit because of their skills in judging grain price movements and marketing opportunities. There may also be scope for well-organized farmer co-operatives, for millers, poultry farmers and industrial users of grain to adopt inventory credit. It is important to avoid viewing marketing credit in the same light as production credit has come to be seen in many parts of Africa, i.e. as a form of entitlement which does not have to be repaid.

This conclusion may initially be unwelcome to those who wish to ensure that maximum benefits accrue directly to farmers. However, two observations are relevant.

- Because of the highly competitive nature of most cereal markets in developing countries, farmers can be expected to benefit from increased purchasing by middlemen, millers and other parties in receipt of inventory credit. By buying more grain at harvest time, they will bid up the market price.
- The best way to give farmers direct access to marketing credit, if so desired, is by helping them organize groups which are perceived by the banks as a good credit risk. Again this requires an end to paternalistic approaches where credit comes to be viewed as an entitlement. TechnoServe's approach (see Case Study 5) is instructive in this regard.

Risks with inventory credit and how to manage them

Lending is about managing risk, and it is important to identify the main risks involved with inventory credit. These seem to be inconsistent government policies, excessive funding on soft terms, the physical security of the produce, certain "legal risks", and speculative loss. Ways of minimizing these risks are discussed below.

☐ Inconsistent government policies

Risks arising from government policies were mentioned in Section 4. If policies are not supportive of inventory financing and they are not applied in a fairly consistent manner, promotion of the concept should be avoided.

The Ghana case suggests that in some countries it may be possible to "manage" these risks by raising public and government awareness about the benefits of inventory credit. This may involve research followed by a conference, involving all parties interested in the subject of trade financing, where the pros and cons of inventory credit are thoroughly explored. If the conference produces a consensus in favour of inventory credit, Government can take several steps which will enhance public confidence that consistent support will be forthcoming:

(a) produce a policy statement in favour of this form of financing, reaffirming its resolve to leave normal trade and trade financing to the private sector, to refrain from internal controls on prices and grain movements, and only to intervene in specified circumstances involving grave threats to food security, in ways which do not create disincentives to private production and trade;

(b) support commercial warehouse development by promptly making available to the private sector redundant state-owned warehouses (see Section 8);

(c) make inventory credit a specific part of the terms of reference of a ministry (or set up an informal task force of ministries, banks and traders), and commission research to assist in its effective implementation;

(d) promote and finance an effective market information system.

❏ Excessive funding on soft terms

The Malian case (Case Study 4) shows that the success of inventory credit can be compromised by the enthusiasm of donors seeking quick results through the provision of credit.

As a general rule, inventory credit is likely to be successful and sustainable when banks lend at their own risk, making use of funds mobilized through local branch networks. However, the Philippines case (Case Study 1) indicates that there are exceptions to this rule in countries with more mature banking systems. In the Philippines, lending risks are underwritten by a Government agency, Quedan and Rural Credit Guarantee Corporation (Quedancor), which guarantees the stock at an official guarantee price. This has not led to irresponsible lending, however, and Quedancor's resources (2 percent of amounts loaned) have easily covered pay-outs.

In many countries, however, such arrangements risk creating an environment where banks can lend irresponsibly. Political pressures may also cause guarantee prices to be set at unrealistically high levels, leading to the bankruptcy of the organization providing the guarantee. Generally speaking, therefore, it is suggested that governments do not offer official guarantees. Banks have much to gain through the successful operation of inventory credit and, preferably, they, rather than governments or donors, should be the prime movers in establishing inventory credit

❏ Physical security of the produce

Most risks involving physical security can be eliminated by making sure the produce is insured against fire and extreme weather conditions (hurricanes, etc.), and by banks working only with competent and highly reputable warehouse operators. However, even where highly reputable companies are involved, there is always scope for human error and the safe-keeping of produce cannot always be taken for granted.

The availability of insurance cover will vary according to the state of the local insurance business, and the general security situation in the country concerned. In Ghana, cover can be obtained for fire at low premiums, 0.2 percent of the value of the produce insured, while a small additional charge will cover whirlwinds and tornadoes.

Guidelines for the selection of warehouse operators were provided in Section 3.

☐ **Legal risks involving the unauthorized sale of produce by the borrower, and the death or bankruptcy of the borrower or the warehouse operator**

The legal risks involved with inventory credit schemes, discussed in greater detail in Annex 2, will differ depending on the legal framework that exists in a particular country. These risks can be divided into two types. The first might be called "substantive" risks, i.e. risks that arise because a country's laws are ambiguous or inconsistent, or because they fail to provide sufficient protection to the interests of the various parties. One risk that is likely to arise in the case of an inventory credit scheme is that the borrower may sell the produce without the lender's authorization. Of course, the lender will still have a right to sue the borrower for breaching the loan agreement, but that right may not be worth much now that the underlying security, i.e. the grain, has gone out of the control of the borrower. Unless the law provides for a procedure for a bank to register its security interest, and also provides that such an interest exists, then the lender may have a hard time taking action to get the grain back from a third party who purchased it in good faith.

Other substantive risks that may be encountered arise in the case of the death or bankruptcy of a borrower or warehouse operator. The question a lender must keep in mind is whether its claim against the asset will survive either event. Ideally, a lender's security interest should provide it "priority" against the claims of other creditors – in other words, even in the case of death or bankruptcy, a secured lender should have first access to the collateral, before the deceased's estate, the bankruptcy court or the trustee gets such access. Unfortunately, laws regarding inheritance and bankruptcy tend to be complex and are often ambiguous, and may at times override the interest of the secured lender. It is important, therefore, to determine the extent of these risks under the laws of a given country, and investigate ways of minimizing them.

In lending to traders, some lenders may wish to expand the range of collateral options by requiring insurance on the life of the trader. Such "key-man" insurance may be justified because grain traders are often "one-man-bands" and their death may seriously jeopardise loan repayment.

The second type of legal risks may be characterized as "procedural" risks. However strong a lender's legal rights may seem on paper, the procedures laid out for realizing those rights may be extremely time-consuming, expensive and full of pitfalls for the unwary. Such factors can be very important, particularly where security for a loan is provided by a perishable commodity like grain. These risks are exacerbated in situations where a country's judicial system is overburdened, weak or corrupt.

☐ Speculative loss

In Section 1 it was mentioned how returns to storage can vary from one year to the next (this is illustrated graphically in Figures A1-A6 in Annex 1). Even in cases where price fluctuations are extreme, such as maize in Ghana, there are years when price rises are relatively modest. Risks are generally greatest in years of bumper crops. The extensive provision of inventory credit will increase these risks. As banks increasingly make funds available for storage, the inter-seasonal price pattern should become smoother and there will be fewer opportunities for profitable trading. The level of speculative risk, and the possibility of banks being forced to realize assets in the form of stock, will increase.

With internationally traded commodities, speculative risks can be avoided by hedging on futures markets. However, this is difficult in the case of the many commodities for which futures markets do not exist or which are produced mainly for local consumption. Prices are often out of line with those in the world at large, so that speculative risks cannot be hedged on futures markets.

While the borrower cannot avoid speculative risks, there is much that the bank can do to minimize its exposure to speculative losses. The following measures are important.

- Thorough scrutiny of loan applicants: as indicated in Section 3, the most important criteria should be the borrower's professionalism and track record in the trade, and credit history, if he or she has one.
- Understanding the trade in the commodity concerned and making full use of market intelligence: the bank may consider appointing a market analyst, possibly on a part-time basis, as discussed in Section 3.
- Involving borrower's equity as a proportion of the grain financed, and adjusting the equity requirement according to perceived risk.
- Establishing a realistic term for the loan which does not go beyond the time when prices can be expected to experience seasonal falls.

Making use of existing public storage capacity

In most countries market liberalization calls for a reduced role for parastatals or state-controlled co-operatives that formerly were the sole official marketing channels. These agencies have large storage capacity, as well as grain dryers and cleaners which are of excellent quality. To date, only a few countries have successfully identified alternative uses for these facilities and seldom have they been sold to the public.

Some grain marketing parastatals may have a future as warehouse operators. Indeed they could be the basis for a network of stores, such as that existing in India, which offers secure storage for a wide range of products. Many parastatals have considerable expertise in storage techniques and pest control. Unfortunately, there can be several problems in using parastatals in this way.

- Some have a reputation for corruption and unexplained leakages. This may result in high insurance premiums and make private traders or banks unwilling to entrust stock to them.
- They lack the political independence to resist seizure of stock by governments when food security crises occur.
- They usually continue to carry out a trading role after liberalization. Coupled with financial difficulties and overstaffing, this can lead to conflicts of interest and poor services to private customers.

The Ghana Food Distribution Corporation (GFDC) is a parastatal which has moved speedily into the storekeeper role and has satisfactorily performed the technical functions involved. Notwithstanding this, GFDC still exhibits some of the typical problems associated with parastatals and this gives legitimate cause for concern (see Case Study 4).

In view of the above problems, serious consideration should be given to the possibility of selling off or leasing stores and grain handling equipment to the private sector. This should be done quickly through a tendering process or other mechanism which ensures that the disposal prices are not inflated but are in line with going market prices.

Another possibility is to put stores in the hands of a specialist public warehousing organization which has no trading role, such as the Central Warehousing Corporation in India (see Case Study 2). However, this option involves some of the same institutional problems of parastatal trading enterprises, and can make it difficult to engender bank confidence. One way in which confidence might be enhanced is for the warehousing corporation simply to maintain the stores and lease them to professional warehouse operators in the private sector.

Section 8
Quality control

This brief discussion on aspects of quality control relates to Africa, although it may be relevant in other parts of the world.

Private sector grain marketing systems rarely employ formal quality control standards, and levels of moisture, foreign matter, broken grains, etc. are often high. However, due to their rapid stock turnover, traders are able to operate in this manner without it adversely affecting their business.

Parastatals usually have formal buying standards for grains and are often well equipped with moisture meters, grain drying and cleaning equipment, but in many countries this equipment is under-used and standards are only vaguely applied.

When grain has to be stored for several months, stricter controls are needed to avoid spoilage, especially regarding moisture content. Moreover, in the event of a dispute between the depositor and the warehouse operator regarding the quality of stock at the time of redemption, there must be an agreement over quality at the time of deposit, so that any deterioration can be measured. Standards are also required if warehouse receipts are to become negotiable, and grain is to be traded by specification, as suggested in Section 4.

For these reasons warehouse operators should establish their own set of quality standards. At first these are likely to be simple standards establishing a Fair Average Quality (FAQ) for food or feed use. Standards can be less exacting when the identity of produce is preserved than when it is confused. As noted previously (see page 16), uniform standards are needed when identity is confused to avoid the situation whereby depositors delivering high-quality produce subsidize those who deliver poor grain.

Warehouse operators need to be fully familiar with scientific storage measures and pest control techniques. Governments, possibly through former parastatals, can provide support in the form of appropriate training. However, the temptation to license warehouse operators should usually be resisted because it often creates opportunities for corruption. Control of warehouse standards will come through the banks, whose funds are tied up in the stock, and the insurance companies, who will not provide insurance if they think that a storekeeper is incompetent.

Fumigation can be a contentious issue, particularly when private storekeepers are involved. Parastatal pest control staff have usually learnt to practise preventative pest control, but a less enlightened commercial attitude is to fumigate only when infestation is rife, as a last resort, to prevent the commodity from dropping a grade or becoming unsaleable. Problems will be reduced if there are clear contracts for fumigation, followed up by regular monitoring of fumigation practice and infestation levels.

Section 9
Future developments which could be based on inventory credit

DEVELOPMENT OF A FUTURES MARKET

In the larger countries of Eastern Europe and the developing world, trading in warehouse warrants may eventually lead to commodity exchanges, with trading on a futures basis. Futures trading is fundamentally different from the physical trading as discussed here. All contracts are for a conventionally standardized grade of commodity, in a standard lot size, and for delivery at a standard day of a month in a standard location. However, a futures trade can only develop where there is an underlying physical trade in the commodity concerned. A trade in warrants helps establish standards for quality and other parameters, upon which the futures trade can be established.

Few futures contracts go through to physical delivery as the volume of transactions is such that sales are normally cancelled out by purchases. However, when delivery does occur, the warehouse warrant is a convenient document by which physical exchange can be registered[7].

Futures transactions are normally separate from physical transactions, and should not be confused with "forward" sales, which are simply physical transactions specifying delivery of the goods at some date in the future. However, the development of futures markets is advantageous to producers, traders and processors, as it allows them all to manage price risks through hedging. Futures markets also allow people outside the physical trade to

---

[7] One of the London commodity exchanges, the London Metal Exchange, also acts as a warehouse operator. It has a series of warehouses with stocks of metal bars which are used in the settlement of contracts going through to delivery.

speculate in the commodity concerned. Futures prices influence physical prices and vice versa, and provide a vital link between the commodity trade and financial markets, and help smooth price fluctuations.

The developing world's experience with such exchanges is rudimentary and not encouraging, particularly with domestically traded commodities. Markets tend to suffer from lack of liquidity, there being a limited number of buyers and sellers interested in the commodity concerned. Consequently, they are more vulnerable to manipulation than are established exchanges. In Brazil, development of futures markets for grain has been hampered by the lack of standardized grades, hindrance to the movement of merchandise and the trade's inability to deliver on contracts. Futures markets should not have been developed:

- while Government retained a price stabilization capacity which removed market operators' incentive to engage in hedging
- wihout first having developed markets for physical trade in the produce concerned.

COMMODITY FUNDS AND COMMODITY CERTIFICATES WITH GUARANTEED DELIVERY

Further innovations in the financial and trading sector in Brazil suggest the sort of developments which are possible in the long term, particularly in the more developed middle-income countries. In July 1992, the Federal Government authorized the establishment of Commodity Investment Funds. These funds raise resources on the market, which must be invested in a range of financial products, of which a minimum of 25 percent and a maximum of 80 percent should be invested in papers backed by agricultural commodities, including warrants, Commodity Certificates with Guaranteed Delivery (CM-Gs – see below) and futures contracts. Any commercial bank can set up a Commodity Fund and Federal and State Governments can buy and sell positions in them.

In their first year of operations, Commodity Funds raised substantial amounts of funds and in September 1993 their capitalization was equivalent to US$4.8 billion. The Funds were on their way to becoming the main vehicle for gathering financial resources for agricultural production and marketing. However, they were running into a problem which had dogged previous attempts to modernize the financing of agricultural trade – the lack of credibility of warehouse warrants.

The Brazilian experience may seem remote to countries whose level of development and/or scale of the internal market does not permit such sophistication in the financial sphere. However, it brings home the fundamental importance of starting the process of improving trade finance with sound storekeepers, whose warrants inspire business confidence.

Brazil is developing another instrument which may partially substitute for the warehouse warrant, the Commodity Certificate with Guaranteed Delivery (CM-G). It is a sales contract on a given commodity and comes in two versions: guaranteed immediate delivery, which refers to existing stocks; and guaranteed future delivery, which refers to crops not yet harvested, or even crops not yet established. CM-Gs are intended to mobilize resources from the market to finance commodity storage and production costs. They would be issued by the owner of the commodity, registered in the clearing-houses of commodity exchanges, and guaranteed by a commercial bank.

The GM-G contracts will be traded on spot markets, and are expected to be the main stock-based paper to be purchased by Commodity Funds, instead of warrants. In countries which are much less developed than Brazil, however, it is difficult to see such financial instruments taking off; there are simply not sufficient creditworthy parties to issue the certificates. A well-organized system of warehouse warrants can, by contrast, provide physical security upon which the financial system can base its confidence. By establishing the credentials of borrowers in the eyes of the banks, inventory credit can be a first step towards creating more sophisticated systems.

Case Study 1
Quedan programme for paddy marketing credit in the Philippines

INTRODUCTION
During the 1970s food production in the Philippines underwent a rapid expansion enabling the country to move from a situation of deficit to self-sufficiency. However, the rapid increase in production proved difficult for the marketing system to handle. In particular, traders were unable to raise operating finance to purchase the crop from farmers. Banks required traders to mortgage property to obtain loans, but working capital could often not be raised in that way as traders' property was already mortgaged to pay for the necessary expansion of milling and storage capacity.

To address this constraint, the Quedan Financing Programme was instituted in 1978, under the auspices of the Quedan Guarantee Fund Board and, in 1992, this organization became the Quedan and Rural Credit Guarantee Corporation (Quedancor). Quedancor was established with an authorized capital stock of P2 billion (about US$80 million) and a broader mandate than its predecessor, to enable it to cover not only inventory financing, but also other types of credit financing in the agriculture sector.

OPERATION OF THE QUEDAN PROGRAMME FOR MILLERS
Franchising
Quedancor carries out a full evaluation of the credit and financial capacity of the paddy millers and traders applying for Quedan-backed inventory credit. The applicants' warehouse facilities are also examined by the National Food Authority (NFA). The NFA absorbs costs associated with inspection, while Quedancor's costs are met partly out of interest on its

capital base and partly by the millers who pay a Guarantee Fee calculated at the rate of 2 percent of borrowed funds per year.

After the evaluation, which usually takes three to four weeks, a decision is made on whether to franchise the miller and, if so, for how many bags the Certificate of Franchise will be granted. This can be as low as 500 bags or as high as 20 000 but will never represent the entire storage capacity of the miller. The Certificate, which is issued by NFA on the advice of Quedancor, entitles the holder to issue warehouse receipts (Quedans) against stocks of his own grain or against stocks of a third party.

The fact that millers can pledge stocks stored on their own premises is a major advantage, as they are spared the cost of transporting paddy to and from independent warehouses. Moreover, the cost of storage in their warehouses is generally lower than commercial storage rates.

Procedures for obtaining loans

Millers seeking franchise certificates for the first time can apply for loans from banks at the same time as they request a Certificate of Franchise. However, many millers have established Certificates and thus apply to one of the accredited banks close to the time the loan is required. For new Certificates the banks will make parallel enquiries regarding the miller's creditworthiness, although they do tend to lean heavily on the recommendation of Quedancor.

Although it takes the banks just a few days to process documents for a Quedan loan, the procedure is more complex, both for the bank and the customer, than for standard loans secured by conventional collateral. The applicant must present to the bank a copy of the Certificate of Franchise, a warehouse receipt, a Stock Inspection Report, an affidavit of stock owner-ship and evidence that the stock is insured. He or she is also required to post a security bond for one-third of the value of the stored stocks. Loans are for up to 180 days for paddy, but for up to only 90 days for other grains. In practice, millers take out loans for a period which is likely to maximize their return from stockholding. Stock is inspected at least twice during a 180-day period by Quedancor officials while it is held in the millers' warehouses.

Guarantee cover and rediscounting

After the loan is released the lending bank applies to Quedancor for guarantee cover. Quedancor guarantees the existence of the stocks used as collateral and undertakes to pay 80 percent of the loan principal plus accrued interest. It does not guarantee the value of the stocks which, theoretically, could fall if excessive supplies were introduced onto the market by the NFA. This possibility is covered by an agreement that all stocks held under Quedan loans will, if necessary, be purchased by NFA on maturity of the loan. In practice this has not happened, the market price always being above the official NFA price during the pre-harvest season.

Banks can immediately rediscount Quedan loans through the Central Bank of the Philippines. A "second window" rediscount rate is offered. In July 1992 this was 18 percent, compared with commercial rates of 24 percent. The full benefit of this spread is not passed on to the trader/miller as the Quedancor Guarantee Fee of up to 2 percent per year of the value of the loan is deducted, together with bank costs, giving an interest rate of 20-21 percent per year.

Loan repayment

On maturity the borrower repays the bank and receives a certificate of loan settlement permitting him to remove the paddy from his warehouse for sale or milling. Early repayment incurs no penalty. Procedures exist to permit stock rotation while maintaining the same franchised quantity in store. Using a device known as a Commodity Trust Receipt, it is even possible for the miller to mill Quedan stocks provided that those stocks are covered by funds in the bank or are guaranteed by the bank.

In the unlikely event of default the bank must file a notice of default within 15 days of the maturity date. An inspection of the miller's warehouse is then carried out by Quedancor, the bank and NFA. Where stocks are found to be missing, procedures are then instituted for Quedancor to reimburse the bank and undertake recovery actions against the miller.

POSITION OF THE BANKS

Banks in the Philippines almost invariably require some sort of collateral as

security when lending to grain millers. Agricultural stocks are unaccept-
able, even if held in bonded warehouses, regardless of the creditworthiness
of the applicant.

Given that Quedan loans attract a repayment rate of around 99 percent,
the reluctance of the banks to deal directly with traders without the benefit
of a Quedancor guarantee or property mortgage is not easy to understand.
This reluctance is partly historical; banks have made significant losses on
loans to the agricultural sector and millers tend to be regarded as part of the
agricultural sector rather than part of the commercial sector. Banks also state
that they lack information on paddy prices and market trends to enable them
to assess the potential viability of a loan against stock.

It was only with some difficulty that the banks were originally persuaded
to take part in the Quedan programme, but 184 are now accredited, ranging
from large organizations with national coverage to small local banks. When
the scheme was set up the banks wanted stocks to be held in NFA
warehouses and only after considerable persuasion did they agree to millers
holding their own stocks.

For the banks, the provision of Quedan loans is now largely risk-free. The
existence of the stocks is guaranteed by Quedancor. The stocks must be
insured by the millers before they can obtain a loan and their value is
guaranteed by NFA.

BENEFITS OF QUEDAN LOANS FOR MILLERS

Millers themselves often extend credit. Farmers are supplied with inputs at
planting time and beyond, while a 30-day payment credit is often provided
to rice retailers. The additional liquidity in the marketing system as a result
of the Quedan scheme increases both the amount of grain which they can
buy from farmers and the funds available for credit.

A small survey of millers operating north of Manila revealed an average
(mean) Quedan franchise of around 10 000 bags and an average milling
capacity of 900 bags a day. Thus a Quedan loan (worth about US$7 per bag
in 1992) in the area surveyed provides millers with operating capital
equivalent to 11 days' milling. In other areas of the country, however, such
loans appear to be responsible for a higher proportion of total milling

capacity. It should be stressed that, immediately after harvest, there is often a surplus of milled rice and millers encounter difficulties in disposing of it. Thus, a Quedan loan, although representing a small part of their total throughput, is made available at an opportune time, assisting them to build up stocks of paddy.

LEGISLATIVE FRAMEWORK
The operation of a guarantee system is underpinned by legislation relating to warehouse deposits. Quedan transactions are governed by a General Bonded Warehouse Act and by a Warehouse Receipts Law.

Under the General Bonded Warehouse Act, an operator of a bonded warehouse (which all Quedan franchise holders are) is required to obtain a licence, to put up a bond, to insure the warehouse contents against theft and fire, to keep complete records of commodities received, receipts issued and withdrawals made, and to forward such documentation to the appropriate Ministry. Failure to comply with his legal obligations, so causing a loss to another party (e.g. Quedancor), renders the warehouse owner liable to civil suits, and criminal prosecution.

Under the Warehouse Receipts Law, the contents of a written warehouse receipt and all other necessary documentation related to receipt and delivery are defined.

EVALUATION OF THE QUEDAN PROGRAMME
The benefits of the Quedan programme are widely believed to be higher prices for farmers immediately after harvest and a strengthening of trader/ millers so that they are able to take over the functions of an increasingly financially strapped NFA, together with less tangible benefits such as better post-harvest handling and an increased exposure of banks to rural areas. Without detailed research it is impossible to confirm that farmer prices are higher, though one consultancy study found that in one area farmgate prices were 7.7 percent higher than they would have been without inventory credit.

When the Quedan programme was set up, it was in response to a lack of capital for traders, but it is not clear whether this remains a constraint. Many millers do not avail themselves of Quedan loans and mortgage their plant for all of their credit requirements.

Millers benefitting from Quedan loans receive two forms of subsidy. Firstly, as indicated above, there is an interest rate subsidy, which although reduced in recent years, is still substantial. Secondly, the loan premium charged by Quedancor does not fully meet the costs of the programme, which are covered by the income from Quedancor's capital. Millers say that they use Quedan loans because of the favourable interest rate **and** because they are not required to mortgage plant and equipment. As they seem to have less problems in finding such collateral than they did when the Quedan scheme was set up, it is not clear whether the latter advantage would motivate millers to use Quedan loans in the absence of the interest rate subsidy.

The NFA buys less than 10 percent of marketed paddy annually. However, its influence on the rice market is somewhat greater than this figure would imply as NFA rice is usually marketed only during the "lean" season, a period of about three months. Thus if the Authority buys 5 percent of the crop in one year, it may market 20 percent of the rice sold in the lean season. NFA involvement in the market tends to squeeze the margins of millers and diminishes the profitability of inter-seasonal storage, but this has usually remained sufficiently profitable to justify the risk of stockholding.

While NFA operates within clearly defined boundaries, millers are able to assess – with a reasonable degree of confidence – the likely returns from long-term storage of paddy. However, the Philippines has sometimes imported rice unexpectedly, or planned exports have not materialized. The consequent additional rice on the market has, on a few occasions, resulted in losses on inter-seasonal storage, although no traders have had to adopt the fall-back position of selling their stock to the NFA at its official buying price. Even when some losses do occur on stocks, those traders who roll over Quedan loans several times in a season are able to compensate for their losses by the increased turnover.

In summary, the Quedan system provides selected, creditworthy millers and traders with a useful channel of credit which facilitates both the procurement of paddy from farmers and inter-seasonal storage. However, given the availability of other sources of finance, the extent to which millers would make use of Quedan loans if there were no interest rate subsidies remains to be seen.

Case Study 2
Agricultural marketing credit in India

INTRODUCTION

The arrangements made for agricultural marketing credit in India provide, on the face of it, the basis for a system which could be replicated in many other countries of the world. The country has a mixed marketing system, with state procurement and distribution accounting for about one quarter of marketed grain and the private sector the remainder. It has an efficient warehousing network run at national and state level, which can provide secure storage with minimal losses. There are appropriate Warehouse Acts and provision for negotiable Warehouse Receipts to be issued which can be used by the trader, miller or farmer to raise loans against deposited stocks.

While the mechanism for providing credit for marketing is in place, it is not widely used by traders and millers. Since the 1940s, Government policy towards both the financial sector and food grain marketing has been more concerned with containing and regulating private initiative than with stimulating it. Most of the commercial banks have been nationalized, they are highly subsidized, and there are multiple restrictions on lending for agricultural trade. There are also restrictions upon the level of food stocks which can be held by the private sector, the purpose of which is to prevent "hoarding". The lessons to be learned from official marketing credit arrangements in India are thus lessons of potential rather than of actual achievement.

FOOD MARKETING IN INDIA

Until 1943 Government rarely intervened in food marketing, but starting in that year a succession of programmes was implemented until 1965, when the Food Corporation of India (FCI) was formed to take over most procurement activities from the Department of Food. Since then, the Corporation has been handling the purchase, storage, movement and distribution of food at national level. Its annual procurement now runs at around 18 million tonnes, equal to about 25 percent of the marketed surplus.

Food procured by FCI, and to a lesser extent by the states themselves, is distributed by the states under the Public Distribution System (PDS). Grain is issued by FCI at a uniform price, to which states add sales taxes and other charges and may subtract an additional subsidy before distribution to consumers through Fair Price Shops and Ration Shops. There is a high element of subsidy involved, estimated at over US$1 billion per year nationally, including losses incurred by FCI.

Grain can enter the market in a number of ways. Farmers can sell directly to traders or millers: an arrangement which often involves an advance payment prior to harvest. Alternatively, direct sale can take place through a commission agent, who is responsible for cleaning and bagging the grain and having it officially weighed, in one of the numerous markets around the country. Sale is either by regulated open auction or by tender. Indirect sale can be made through middlemen in the villages. Most communities have brokers who will buy from farmers for sale to traders. Often they advance funds to farmers for input supply and other purposes. Grain millers and traders tend to form closely knit groups; they are almost all organized into associations and some groups operate co-operative banks.

In addition to procurement by FCI and public distribution by the states, the operation of a free grain market is constrained in many other ways. Traders allege that they have to be aware of around 18 different Acts and Regulations. The exact meaning of these can be difficult to find out and they tend to change frequently. There is often contradiction between national and state regulations. There does, however, appear to be a move to liberalize grain marketing, in concert with the general liberalization of the Indian economy now taking place.

SOURCES OF MARKETING CREDIT AVAILABLE TO TRADERS
Inventory credit using warehouse deposits
Traders in wheat, paddy and rice, together with wheat and rice millers have, in theory, the opportunity to obtain credit from banks against stocks

deposited in warehouses, which will normally be those operated by the Central Warehousing Corporation (CWC) or by state warehousing corporations. The storage of food crops is carried out at favourable rates and is being subsidized by revenue from the storage of industrial products.

Credit against stocks held in the traders' own stores

Traders with long-standing relationships with a bank and a reputation for reliability can hypothecate stock held on their own premises (this is similar to the Philippine case described in Case Study 1). It is instructive to examine some of the features of this arrangement, though it should be noted that due to the above-mentioned credit restrictions, it is rarely used in practice.

The bank either places the stock under lock and key or, alternatively, inspects it on a regular basis. A major advantage to the borrower is that the pledged stock does not have to be moved to and from the warehouse and it can be rotated, i.e. it can be milled or sold on a first-in-first-out basis. Moreover, the value of the loan is not necessarily fixed but may be subject to a "cash credit limit" based on the maximum stock (subject to stockholding regulations) that the trader wishes to maintain. A disadvantage of this arrangement is that loans may take slightly longer to arrange.

Private and informal sources

Many traders can fund their operations from their own equity, particularly since the extent of these operations is constrained by stockholding limits. Others can raise money on India's highly developed informal credit markets at rates of interest between 3 and 8 percent greater than the prevailing bank rate. Sometimes such loans are made against negotiable warehouse receipts. Traders will often lend short-term funds or "call" money to each other.

INVENTORY CREDIT AVAILABLE TO FARMERS

All farmers have the option of seeking credit against warehouse receipts, subject to the same constraints as apply to traders. However, in practice, they make only limited use of these facilities, and when they store in warehouses it is often for their own consumption, and not for trading purposes. Discharging inventory loans can be difficult because traders are reluctant to go through all the procedures required (i.e. inspecting the grain at the warehouse, paying the bank, receiving the warehouse receipt and then collecting the grain), when they can more easily procure similar produce from farmers at the local market.

As a result of these difficulties, some co-operatives have introduced schemes whereby farmers can receive advances on crops deposited in warehouses situated in or adjacent to government-regulated markets. When the farmer wishes to sell, his produce is auctioned, the loan repayment and costs are deducted and he is paid the excess. This appears to be an attractive system, but its widespread use is constrained by a shortage of appropriate storage space close to markets.

For small (up to 2 acres: 0.8 hectares) and marginal (2-5 acres: 0.8-2 hectares) farmers, special Produce Marketing Loan Schemes apply which provide marketing credit at lower interest rates than paid by traders and permit on-farm storage. In most areas of the country farmers can obtain marketing loans of a maximum of R5 000[1] for a period of up to six months. This maximum sum has remained unchanged for 12 years and now represents just 25 100-kg bags of wheat or 11 bags of paddy, as loans are based on 75 percent of the official procurement price. These loans are available only to farmers who have taken out production loans. Eighty-two of the 360 districts in the country have been chosen as Special Foodgrain Production Areas where the maximum loan has been increased to R10 000 or twice the production loan, whichever is the lesser. In 1990, when supplies were short, the scheme was suspended for a season in order to encourage more production to come onto the market.

OPERATION OF BANK ADVANCES AGAINST WAREHOUSE RECEIPTS

Warehouse receipts can be either negotiable or non-negotiable. Space on warehouse receipts is provided for recording quantities deposited and quantities released. The warehouse operator must insure all stocks deposited (based on the value at the time of deposit) and, upon presentation of the receipt, release the same quality and quantity of goods as deposited, subject

---

[1]Exchange rate (early 1993): R28 = US$1

to natural storage loss. The CWC and other warehousing organizations keep the deposits of each farmer/trader separate, there being no question of combining them in one big stack. Preservation of the identity of the grain, inevitably, leads to inefficient use of warehouse space as some farmers may deposit just a few bags and, combined with the favourable storage rates charged for agricultural produce, means that agricultural depositors are effectively subsidized by those using the warehouses for industrial purposes.

A trader or farmer seeking a bank advance endorses the receipt to the bank which then informs the warehouse operator that it has a lien on the receipt through the issuance of a "Notice of the Bank's Lien of Specified Goods". When the loan is cleared, in full or in part, the bank sends a letter requesting delivery from the warehouse and this is submitted by the depositor, together with the endorsed warehouse receipt. If the depositor fails to clear the loan within the stipulated time the bank has the right to sell the stock; often it will request the warehouse operator to do this on its behalf.

The use of warehouse receipts for bank advances requires the existence of appropriate legislation governing the use of the receipts and setting out the responsibilities of the warehouse operator. The following are some of the salient points from Indian legislation.

- Provision is made for receipts to be negotiable and to entitle the lawful holder of the receipt access to the goods on the same terms and conditions as the person who originally deposited them.
- Procedures are specified for the replacement of a Warehouse Receipt which has been lost, defaced, damaged, destroyed or torn.
- Procedures are specified should the depositor die.
- The duties and responsibilities of the warehouse operator are specified; the operator may refuse to accept a deposit if the goods are in a condition not likely to stand storage.
- The treatment of deteriorating goods is specified.
- Provision is made for the settlement of disputes relating to loss or damage of the stock.

RESTRICTIONS ON THE PROVISION OF MARKETING CREDIT

The Reserve Bank of India (RBI) issues periodic instructions to the banks regarding the overall level of credit to be made available and regarding priority sectors. Trading in agricultural crops has relatively low priority.

All loans against stock are subject to the Selective Credit Control Act. Under this Act the RBI is able to vary the use of credit for marketing purposes by controlling the overall level of credit, the margin that the borrower must fund from his own resources, and the rate of interest. In addition there are marketing restrictions relating to the levels of stocks which may be held by the private sector.

Credit margins

The main method employed by RBI to control private sector access to trade credit is the adjustment of the loan margin. The margin refers to the percentage of the value of the crop being pledged or mortgaged by the farmer, miller or trader which cannot be loaned by the bank. Thus where a margin of 40 percent applies, banks can lend 60 percent of the value (i.e. the official procurement price) of the pledged stock.

While the margins applied to farmers are relatively low, at 25 percent, those which apply to traders are high and do not appear to offer any significant incentive for a trader to seek a loan. The margin for traders permits them to obtain loans equivalent to 25 percent of the value of their hypothecated stock and 40 percent of the value of stock supported by warehouse receipts.

Margins are adjusted periodically by RBI according to prevailing market conditions. The assumption underlying the adjustments is that an increase in the margin will force traders to sell part of their stock in order to comply with the new conditions. For example, a miller borrowing R100 000 when the margin is 50 percent will be entitled to borrow only R80 000 on the same level of stock when the margin is increased to 60 percent. The miller is therefore forced either to increase his stocks to a level which can support a loan of R100 000 (when he may fall foul of stockholding restrictions) or immediately pay back R20 000 of the advance. It is assumed the miller will do this by selling part of his stock.

RBI conducts studies of food availability throughout the year and adjusts margins accordingly. If supplies are tight margins are increased while if food is abundant the margins are relaxed. Where changes are made to the margins these are required to be implemented "with immediate effect", the intention being to have sudden impact on the state of the market. Inevitably, however, the concept of immediacy is diluted by the time it takes to inform banks of margin changes and the time the banks take to inform their clients. Failure on the part of the borrower to adjust the loan when requested results in the imposition of "penal" interest rates.

It is uncertain whether the RBI's intervention has any effect on the market – there have been no studies to determine impact. The basis for intervention may be that banks do not wish to be seen to be doing anything that might encourage "hoarding", rather than any practical effect that margin changes may have. Moreover, it is likely that traders seeing potential profits by stockholding will be undeterred by margin changes and will, instead, seek funds from the private/informal market.

Interest rates

Interest rates are set by the RBI according to the sector receiving the loan and the size of the loan. At the beginning of January 1993 the rates of interest charged for foodgrains, pulses and oilseeds ranged from 12 percent for loans up to R5 000 to 17.25 percent for loans above R25 000. While the RBI has some flexibility to set rates charged to the agriculture sector, margin adjustment is its main tool in controlling the grain market.

Stockholding levels

Stockholding levels are set by State Governments, which are responsible for their enforcement, in consultation with the Ministry of Food at national level. Authorized levels at the beginning of 1993 varied but in most states were around 250 bags of 100 kg of paddy and 1 000 bags of wheat or rice. Fortnightly inspections are conducted at mills and at the premises of traders to verify stocks.

Inevitably, the private sector has developed ways of avoiding these controls, e.g. by holding stock in the names of others or by purchasing from the farmer but allowing him to retain title until such time as the trader requires the crop. Clearly, however, it is not possible for the trader or miller to borrow money against stocks held in such unofficial ways. Thus the official stock levels effectively establish a maximum amount that a trader can borrow from banks.

CONCLUSIONS

The Indian system has certain features of interest to those seeking to introduce inventory credit into other countries. However in India itself, the scope for inventory credit is restricted by Federal and State Governments' preference for a high level of official control, both with regard to food marketing and the financial sector. Detailed analysis of the pros and cons of such interventionist policies is beyond the scope of this study. Suffice it to say that they are likely to have negative effects in terms of: market efficiency, for example, by decreasing competition in rice marketing; and unnecessarily high costs to Government of supporting both the public distribution system and a heavily subsidized banking sector.

If and when the grain market in India is liberalized, increasing attention will probably be paid to capital requirements of the grain marketing sector, and the country will be fortunate in already having in place appropriate mechanisms for providing advances against stock.

Case Study 3

Financing trade and storage in Mali

In Mali, cereal market liberalization was managed by the Cereals Market Restructuring Programme (PRMC), which was set up jointly by Government and donors. While, overall, Mali's liberalization has achieved considerable success, this is no more than partially true for the trade financing component.

In order to compensate for the reduced role of the parastatal l'Office des Produits Agricoles du Mali (OPAM), credit schemes were set up in 1987 and 1988 to assist both traders and farmers in the procurement and inter-seasonal storage of grain. Funds were channelled through the branches of five banks.

SCHEME FOR TRADERS

With traders, several mechanisms were used to ensure repayment, particularly the use of inventory as collateral. There were two main lines of credit, the "wholesaler line", to assist larger traders handling over 1 000 tonnes of cereals per year, and the "semi-wholesaler" line, assisting those handling less than 1 000 tonnes. The stock was placed in warehouses operated by storekeepers (*tiers détenteurs*) which, according to the Malian Warehousing Law, had to be authorized by the Ministry of Commerce.

The banks then made loans against the presentation of warehouse receipts. Semi-wholesalers were also required to purchase a cash bond, equivalent to a certain proportion of the value of the loan, prior to obtaining the loan. They were also required to associate into groups (Groupements d'Interêt Economiques) to receive credit, making members jointly and severally liable.

The quantities of grain stored with loans to traders and farmers have normally been modest, but in one year (1988/89) they represented a substantial proportion of the total marketed volume (about 12 percent). However, the impact was not altogether as intended. This was a major surplus year and the extra purchasing activity prevented the market from "bottoming out" in its normal fashion. After the loans were used up, prices again fell, with the result that for 18 months, farmers and traders were unable to dispose of their stock without financial loss. This required the due date on the loans to be rolled forward for another year, and some traders (and farmers) experienced significant physical losses due to inadequate storage arrangements.

Overall the recovery of loans has been slow and incomplete. The incentive for traders to repay was diminished by the mechanism which allowed them to avoid investing their own equity in stored grain. Credits were given in tranches, based on 100 percent of the current market value of the grain, in advance of delivery to the storekeeper. By misappropriating the last tranche traders could offset their original investment in the cash bond.

There were many difficulties in administering the schemes. Processing of loans was extremely slow and traders had to wait a month or more to obtain credits. Two storekeepers participated in the scheme, and neither performed satisfactorily. This diminished the commitment of the banks, whose performance was itself negligent, failing to manage the lending risk and failing to pursue unpaid debts. Banks might have performed better had their own funds been invested, but until 1991/92 the schemes were funded entirely with donor money. In the event they simply administered the schemes on behalf of Government without ever having any real sense of ownership.

The wholesaler line of credit was abandoned in 1991. After poor repayment in the 1992/93 season, the same was being considered for the semi-wholesaler line.

SCHEME FOR FARMERS

The PRMC channelled funds through the Agricultural Development Bank (BNDA) which provided one-year credits to Village Associations for procuring grain (millet, sorghum, maize and rice) and storing it for sale in the lean season. The Associations are all-village organizations of farmers, where membership is conferred simply by residing in the village. Unlike build up an individually based equity capital which the member may withdraw upon leaving the Association. In this case, the stock was not used as security, but there was a sort of village guarantee, i.e. the village's future access to credits was conditional upon repayment.

Up to the 1990/91 season the PRMC had lent the Village Associations FCFA1.7 billion (about US$6.2 million). Of this 77 percent had been repaid by 31 January 1992 (see Table 1). The loans have yielded significant benefits, particularly to farmers in mono-crop surplus producing zones who had traditionally experienced cash-flow problems, and who had been able to sell at higher prices in the immediate post-harvest period. However, much of the credit was poorly targeted at districts with little need for this form of credit, and at weak associations. Non-repayment is largely on account of misappropriation by village leaders.

The weakness of many Village Associations appears to be due to the heterogeneity of their all-village membership and the diversity of the interests which have to be represented, including surplus producers, deficit producers, and households of different occupations and ethnic origins. This exacerbates "free-rider" problems which typically affect co-operative-type organizations, and leadership tends to gravitate towards those in existing village and civil hierarchies. According to well-informed sources, members are typically apathetic and are poorly informed by their leaders. Where repayment records have been good this can largely be attributed to two factors: heavy and probably unsustainable supervision by development

TABLE 1
Mali: PRMC credits disbursed and unpaid, to 31 January 1992

Type of client	Year began	Total value disbursed to 1991 - approx (US$ millions)	Percentage unpaid to 31 Jan 1992
Wholesale traders	1986/87	4.7	17
Semi-wholesale traders	1987/88	3.0	13
Farmers organized into Village Associations	1988/89	6.2	23

Note: PRMC also provided a loan guarantee so that conventional marketing credit could be extended from the traditional clientele, consisting of parastatal companies, to private traders, but this facility was withdrawn in 1990.

factors: heavy and probably unsustainable supervision by development organizations; and the village guarantee referred to above, which affected the entire village's future access to bank credit.

It is concluded that in some cases there is good cause for supporting collective storage by farmers, but it should not be a generalized prescription. In a country where the State no longer seeks to stabilize farm revenues, assistance to Village Associations has been successful in shifting the responsibility for this to the farmers themselves. However, it is increasingly recognized in Mali that the groups most likely to succeed will have a common purpose, e.g. in marketing surplus produce, rather than be village-wide organizations whose members have a variety of interests.

OBSERVATIONS ON "TARGETING"

One other lesson from the Malian schemes is that mechanisms for targeting credit at particular kinds of trader, or at farmers in preference to traders, can easily prove futile.

The criteria for being a "semi-wholesaler", as opposed to a "wholesaler", were widely evaded. It might have been simpler to make loans self-targeting, by setting interest rates at a level which would discourage traders who could already obtain unsecured loans or who had sufficient bank collateral of other forms.

A similar observation can be applied to the PRMC's policy of delaying the disbursement of loans to traders until after the Village Associations had been funded, to prevent farmers from "overselling" their produce. Such policies interfere with the banks' lending decisions and, by preventing traders from procuring early in the season when prices are cheapest, diminish their contribution to price stabilization. The PRMC appears to have been caught between two contradictory objectives, on the one hand to get the market processes moving and, on the other, to protect farmers from their operation.

Case Study 4

"Action-research" on trade financing in Ghana

In Ghana, NRI has promoted the financing of the maize trade through inventory credit, and sought to apply lessons learnt in Mali. The term "inventory" credit was, however, already familiar in Ghana, because of a scheme the NGO TechnoServe had been organizing with farmer co-operatives (see next Case Study). NRI's approach was conceived as a complementary initiative, which would make this form of credit available on a much wider scale to whoever could make good use of it. While not being targeted at small farmers, it was designed to benefit them by reducing inter-seasonal price variability.

Two basic principles were to be emphasized: profitability and confidence. Inventory financing should be promoted as a potentially profitable activity to help banks increase their clientele, and capture deposits from the informal trading sector. The role for Government would be to provide a consistent policy framework where banks would feel more confident about lending their ordinary funds. Reliable storekeepers were to be found, so that the banks could ensure the physical security of produce pledged as security.

FEASIBLITY STUDY

A feasibility study, carried out in March-April 1993, showed that there were extraordinarily high inter-seasonal price fluctuations in the maize belt of Brong-Ahafo region, with prices in the two highest months averaging 120 percent above the two lowest months, in real terms. Traders rarely stored grain for more than a few weeks, and this was attributed to their lack of contact with the banks, and the impact of earlier Government policies, which made them afraid that stocks would be seized on the grounds that they were "hoarding". The Ghanaian maize system was studied, and different categories of farmers and traders were categorized according to their potential as customers for inventory credit.

BUILDING CONSENSUS
In early May 1993, a Seminar was organized by the Ministry of Agriculture, with the support of the Overseas Development Administration (ODA) and the World Bank, and interested parties were invited, including Government officials, banks, traders, maize farmers, poultry farmers, TechnoServe and two candidates for the storekeeping role. These were the Ghanaian subsidiary of the multinational inspection company Société Général de Surveillance (Ghana) Ltd (SGS), which was already operating warehouses in the ports, and the Ghana Food Distribution Corporation (GFDC), the grain trading parastatal. GFDC had a network of modern silo facilities but, having exhausted its working capital, was unable to fill them, and was therefore interested in a new role as a supplier of grain drying, cleaning and storage services.

The outcome of the Seminar was an enthusiastic acceptance of the inventory credit concept as presented by NRI and a number of interested parties present, particularly the banks, agreed to implement the proposals. No external funding was to be provided by donors, as banks were considered already to have sufficient liquidity to start lending. NRI was to carry out occasional monitoring.

PILOT IMPLEMENTATION
A cautious and sound start was made in the 1993/94 season, and three traders received loans worth approximately US$310 000, directly or indirectly as a result of the pilot activity. Loans were initially provided by the Government-owned Agricultural Development Bank (ADB), with GFDC acting as collateral manager. Initially ADB lent to a single trader and, as this pilot scheme was successful, financed a second trader late in the season, taking a charge on real estate, but with the commitment that inventory credit would be provided in the next season.

An unforeseen development is that one trader borrowed from a discount house, whose main business is to trade in Treasury Bills. The loan was unsecured, and bore an interest rate significantly in excess of the rate applied by ADB. The operation was favourable in terms of its speediness and the lack of paper work but, due to the high interest rate, ultimately proved burdensome to the borrower, who subsequently sought ADB funding.

A summary of the situation at the end of the first season is shown in Table 2. A comparison of progress in the first and second years, at mid season, is shown in Table 3.

TABLE 2
Statistics of first year of commercial inventory credit, to 31 July 1994, Ghana

	1993/94 season to 31 July
Number of traders having received inventory credit/related financing	3
Other traders being considered for lending	2
Volume of lending (inventory credit and associated loans) in US$	310 000
Volume of grains purchased with credit (tonnes)	5 730
Volume of grain stored under loan (tonnes)	1 055
Number of financial institutions involved in lending	2
Number of other institutions planning to lend in the next season	1
Number of active warehouse operators	1
Loan defaults, bad debts to date	none

TABLE 3
Statistics of first and second year of commercial inventory credit, to January 1995, Ghana

	1993/94 season to March	1994/95 season to January
Number of traders having received inventory credit/related financing	1	11*
Volume of grains stored by traders under loan (tonnes)	1 055	1 477 †
Number of financial institutions involved in lending	1	2
Number of active warehouse operators	1	2

*Six of these traders work together as a group represented by a single borrower.
†The quantity shown should be treated as a minimum as information was not obtained on grain stored by all traders.

The volume of grains stored by traders in receipt of loans was small, about 0.3 percent of the country's marketed surplus (estimated at about 320 000 tonnes). However, the total purchased by these traders was much larger, equivalent to nearly 2 percent of this surplus. Over half of this grain was sold to GFDC, which itself sold on contract to the World Food Programme (WFP), for refugees in the north of Ghana. The remainder was almost entirely sold to poultry farmers.

By financing the traders, ADB has, in effect, assisted the parastatal in completing a contract with the WFP. ADB has also provided the working capital for GFDC, so that its purchases have involved an addition to the Corporation's debt. At the same time, GFDC has acted as collateral manager for the traders.

This situation, with the parastatal carrying out two roles, is at odds with the concept originally promoted (see approach (a) in Section 2). Nevertheless, the overall impact has been positive. In the absence of the scheme, the Government of Ghana would have been relatively unprepared for the food emergency, and is likely to have used food aid from overseas. Without the new lending facilities, the traders would have made less than a quarter of their actual level of purchases. At the same time, the activity seems to have made a minor contribution to price stabilization, with farmers observing an increase in maize prices arising from increased purchases by traders in receipt of loans.

Of longer-term significance is the growing interest of banks and traders. Barclays Bank of Ghana Ltd. entered the field in the 1994/95 season, providing an alternative to ADB. By January 1995, a total of 10 traders had received credit from the two bank and, despite a poor harvest, the amount of grain being stored under loan was up by 50 percent. Given Barclays' satisfaction with its pilot initiative, the stage is set for substantially increased lending in 1995/96.

Maize has been the main commodity stored, but traders are also storing dried anchovies and cowpeas. A proposal has also been formulated for the use of inventory credit in the financing of private procurement of Ghana's main agricultural export, cocoa, but has not so far been implemented.

MAIN ISSUES ARISING
Issues concerning banks
Certain issues have arisen.

- Borrowers' complaints about slow operating procedures – these are particularly irksome when buying crops with a strong seasonal price pattern, and when a week's delay can mean that the borrower is illiquid at the time when prices are most favourable.
- Ground rules requiring traders to provide real estate as complementary collateral before lending against inventory – the banks have shown greater flexibility on this matter in the 1994/95 season.
- Some bank officials indicated reluctance to finance traders when they do not have a firm sales contract for the goods stored – given the informal nature of most maize trading, this seems unreasonably restrictive.

These issues appear to be teething problems. Inventory lending is a new activity in Ghana, involving significant speculative risk. Banks need time to work out ground rules and procedures tailored to the needs of this business, and need to disseminate them to their branch staff. Competition for good customers is forcing them to become more flexible in their approach.

The macro-economic situation also affects banks' initiative in developing new forms of lending. With a high level of Government debt, banks have found the market for Treasury Bills to be extremely remunerative, and this may somewhat dampen their enthusiasm for new forms of lending. Concerns about GFDC (see below) are an additional factor.

Issues concerning warehouse operators
GFDC initially tried hard to market its services, with the support of ADB which has broadcast its willingness to fund farmers and traders storing in GFDC facilities. SGS (Ghana) Ltd., also publicized its services, and in the 1994/95 season started holding stock for borrowers dealing with Barclays Bank. No other parties have put themselves forward for the storekeeping role. GFDC's network of silo sites equipped with dryers and cleaners, in good working order, places it at a competitive advantage to all potential competitors.

GFDC seems to have performed well technically, but less satisfactorily in other aspects. Being a State-owned enterprise and the traders' largest single customer, and having a near monopoly in providing grain drying and cleaning services, it has considerable power *vis-à-vis* the borrowers. This was illustrated by the ease with which .it delayed payment to one of the traders in early 1994, and by the large weight deductions applied in the drying of grain for other parties. In late 1994 there was a major dispute with traders about access to drying facilities, at a time when GFDC was using the facilities to supply its own customers. One trader blamed GFDC for causing damage to 130 tonnes of grain.

GFDC has two business activities. Its long-standing business is commercial, involving the buying and selling of maize on its own account. Due to lack of working capital, its main customer is now the WFP, which buys maize in exchange for imported rice by barter. Its other business is the provision of services (i.e. drying, cleaning and storage) to private sector clients; this has developed in the last two years as a result of the inventory credit initiative. Service business can potentially sustain GFDC in the long term, but only needs a small proportion of the 800 staff who presently work for the corporation. Meanwhile, the viability of GFDC's commercial activities is heavily dependent upon a continuation of major contracts with the WFP. Such continuity is unlikely, given the apparently transitory nature of the country's food emergencies, and the increasing ability of private traders to supply the WFP direct, without going through GFDC.

NRI's previous observations demonstrate that GFDC has a serious conflict-of-interest between its service activities and its commercial activities, with the former sometimes being sacrificed for the latter. This threatens the confidence of traders and bankers in the inventory credit programme. In response to this, two recommendations were made:

- GFDC, traders and their bankers should meet to work out a mode of operation which will enhance the efficiency and transparency in the utilization of the public facilities.
- GFDC service operations should be hived off into a separate entity or entities, with no commercial role, and then be privatized within a framework which ensures efficient and socially desirable utilization.

CONCLUSIONS

Given the background of previous policies, and the time required to bring about sustainable improvements in agricultural financing, overall progress is highly encouraging. While only 11 traders have so far participated, considerable progress has been achieved without any funding by, or loan guarantees from, donors and for this reason is all the more likely to be sustainable. Given the fact that both banks' pilot lending initiatives have (so far) proved successful, there are good prospects for a substantial increase in lending in the 1995/96 season.

Of even greater significance is the fact that the inventory credit initiative has brought about a major change in official policies towards the private grain trade. Until 1993, there was widespread apprehension about the role of private traders, but they are now regarded as vital links between the producer and consumer, who need to be encouraged so as to make markets work more efficiently. This is evident both in the public statements of officials and, notwithstanding the problems noted above, the the way in which private traders are making increasing use of public storage facilities which in the past were reserved for public stocks.

At the same time the success of traders who have obtained inventory credit seems to be having a snowball effect, with the appearance of more traders operating on a relatively large scale. Hitherto, the trade has been dominated by illiterate or semi-illiterate traders who, due to their small scale of operation, have not contributed to inter-seasonal storage. By contrast, some of the new entrants have higher education and technical expertise in the grain trade, making them better able to ensure proper post-harvest handling and delivery against the specifications of larger buyers. Anecdotal information from farmers and traders indicates that the arrival of these larger-scale traders is bidding up on-farm prices[2].

Nevertheless, as indicated above, there are hurdles to be crossed. The long-term impact depends largely upon the approach adopted by the banks,

---

[2]This does not mean that that the only traders responding to the inventory credit initiative are literate and highly educated. Of the 11 borrowers in 1994/95, a group of 6 came from the informal sector.

and upon continued Government support, particularly its willingness to sort out the problems in GFDC and encourage the development of competitive storekeeping services in the private sector.

Case Study 5
TechnoServe's experience with inventory credit for farmers in Ghana

Starting in 1988 the NGO, TechnoServe, working closely with the Department of Co-operatives and the Agricultural Development Bank (ADB), has been encouraging small farmers to form co-operatives in order to avail themselves of inventory credit with which to store their members' crop, primarily maize, for sale at higher prices in the lean season. ADB provides loans against the members' stock, at 75-80 percent of the current market price. The grain is stored in a co-operatively owned and managed warehouse, under the dual-key system, with the co-operative holding one key and TechnoServe or ADB the other.

The co-operatives are promoted along classical, voluntary lines. TechnoServe seeks to create genuine member-controlled organizations, and to avoid using loans and hand-outs to obtain quick and superficially impressive results in the field. Before co-operatives obtain loans they are required to demonstrate their commitment by holding regular meetings, registering their co-operative, generating equity funds, and keeping accounts and minutes of meetings.

Since 1992, TechnoServe has concentrated its efforts on 17 farmer groups in Brong-Ahafo, Eastern and Central Regions. Table 4 shows a statistical summary of the programme and of TechnoServe's estimates of the resulting benefits to farmers.

The volume of credit more than doubled between 1992/93 and 1993/94, but fell back in 1994/95 as a result of a poor harvest. Those co-operatives which have used the facility have gained large benefits, and all loans have been repaid. In 1993/94, TechnoServe reported farmers gaining incremental net benefits of 68 percent from their maize sales, and an overall incre-

TABLE 4
TechnoServe's inventory credit programme in Ghana

	1992/93	1993/94	1994/95
Credits in 000s US$	33.2	52.3	7.1
Number of groups	5	12	6
Maize stored (tonnes)	200	600	111
Repayment by due date (%)	100	100	*
Average cash/bag:			
for participants (US$)	16.57	12.68	*
for non-participants	12.18	7.56	*
Net incremental benefits:			
in US$	4.39	5.13	*
in percentage terms (%)	36	68	*
Average bags per farmers	14	19	*
Incremental income (%)	9	22	*

* indicates data not available
Note:Values have been converted from local currency using exchange rates from international statistics published by IMF.
Source: BOAFO (TechnoServe's Ghana Newsletter), December 1994, and personal communication with TechnoServe staff.

mental income of 22 percent. Part of the reason for this success is that TechnoServe reoriented its efforts towards Ghana's key surplus area, the "maize triangle" of Brong-Ahafo Region, which is the same area where traders in receipt of inventory credit have also concentrated their activity.

Notwithstanding the emphasis on self-reliance, these impressive achievements have involved considerable outside supervision, and assistance in co-ordinating sales. Many of them would probably not survive without this continuing support. Building strong local co-operatives is a difficult process. There are significant problems of mistrust between villagers, member apathy and, last but not least, the negative effect of past hand-outs and debt-forgiveness by other organizations. Persuading farmers to put their equity into schemes has been a continuing difficulty.

One of TechnoServe's answers to this is to encourage them to move into downstream processing of crops. It is believed that farmers will co-operate more actively if they have a business which keeps them working together throughout the year. There have been significant storage problems, but thanks to outside assistance, physical losses were reported to have been contained at three percent. TechnoServe's other main initiative has been to organize oilseed processing co-operatives, and here it is also planned to include an inventory credit component.

Inter-seasonal variability in grain prices: African evidence

In Figures A1 to A6, price data are analysed for the major coarse grain staples in surplus producing areas in three countries: Mali, Ghana and Tanzania. The locations chosen are markets where traders seeking to engage in inter-seasonal storage are likely to procure grain. Price series have been deflated by the consumer price index, except in Mali[1] where inflation was running at about 1 percent per year up to 1994.

The following observations can be made on the basis of the data for Tanzania, Ghana and Mali.

(a) In all three countries the level of inter-seasonal price variability is itself highly variable. In Dioila (Mali) lean-season prices did not rise in one of the three years shown, while in another year they reached 120 percent above lean-season prices. Similar variability is also evident in the detailed data reported by Berg and Kent (1991). In Techiman (Ghana), price variability over a seven-year period has ranged from a low in 1988/89, when May/June prices were between 5 percent and 35 percent above those in the previous September, to a high in 1991/92, when the difference was between 205 percent and 230 percent. In Iringa (Tanzania), the increase in inter-seasonal prices between October and March has been very low in three years (between 10 percent and 25 percent), moderate in two years (30 percent to 55 percent), and very high in one year (150 percent).

---

[1] A weakness of the Malian data is that open-market wholesale prices have only been collected since 1989. For this reason it is supplemented by data for other Sahelian countries collected by Berg and Kent, 1991 (see Table A1).

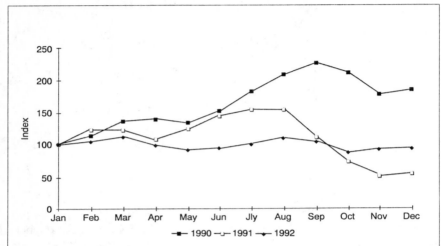

Source: OPAM Market Information System, Mali

FIGURE A1
Monthly wholesale sorghum prices relative to January for 1990-92, Dioila, Mali

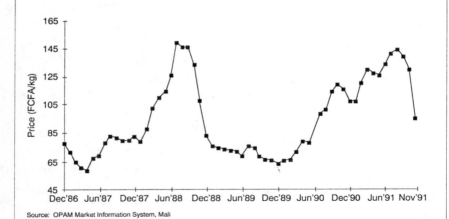

Source: OPAM Market Information System, Mali

FIGURE A2
Monthly average millet prices (retail) for December 1986-November 1991, Mali

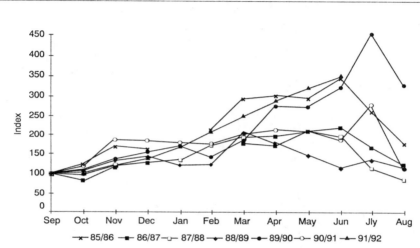

Source: Ministry of Food and Agriculture, Ghana

FIGURE A3
Monthly wholesale maize prices relative to September for 1985-92, Techiman, Ghana

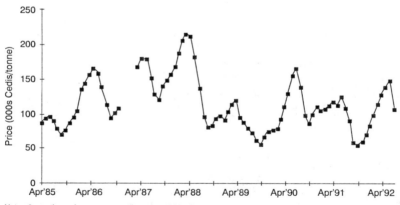

Note: 3-month moving averages adjusted to 1992 prices

Source: Ministry of Food and Agriculture, Ghana

FIGURE A4
Monthly wholesale maize prices for April for1985-92, Techiman, Ghana

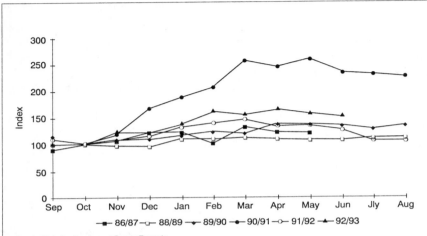

Source: Marketing Development Bureau, Tanzania

FIGURE A5
Monthly wholesale maize prices relative to September for 1986-93, Iringa, Tanzania

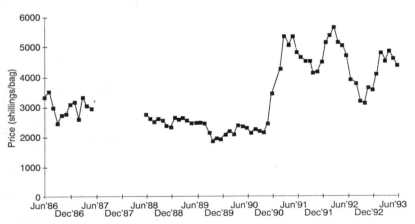

Note: Prices adjusted to June 1993

Source: Marketing Development Bureau, Tanzania

FIGURE A6
Wholesale maize prices per bag for June and December, 1986-93 (June), Iringa,
Tanzania

(b) Prices do not always fall in the same month. For example, in Ghana, prices usually reach their highest levels in May and June, but in two years they peaked in July. This may reflect the trade's expectations of the availability of grain in the forthcoming harvest.

(c) Average price variability is by far the greatest in Ghana, where real prices in May/June have been 120 percent above those in the previous September. Even if allowance is made for an assumed high moisture content at harvest time (about 20 percent), the price increase is still about 110 percent per year. By contrast, Berg and Kent's figures (Table A1) show average price increases for Sahelian rural markets to be only 31 percent. Farmers or traders storing millet or sorghum would have obtained average annual returns on capital invested in excess of 15 percent in only

TABLE A1
Returns to inter-seasonal storage in rural markets

Rural market	Number of years of data	Average price rise between harvest and lean season (6-8 months) (FCFA)	Av. annual return at various costs of capital (%) 0%	15%	40%
Burkina					
Po	8	33	50	35	10
Sanmtenga	6	17	11	-4	-29
Ziniare	4	13	8	-7	-32
Senegal					
Louga	3	20	13	-2	-27
St Louis	3	12	6	-9	-34
Tamba	3	47	49	34	9
Chad					
Mao	3	56	66	51	26
Bousso	3	58	72	57	32
Niger					
Bouza	3	45	45	30	5
Loga	3	46	47	32	7
Maine Soroa	3	14	5	-10	-35
Matamaye	3	39	29	14	-11
Quallam	3	7	0	-15	-40
Average		31	16	16	-9

Notes: Grain is purchased at its average price in the post-harvest period (October, November, December); grain is stored for 6-8 months in a warehouse; and grain is resold at its average price in the lean season period (June, July, August). Physical storage costs include 50 FCFA/bag/month and a 5 percent physical loss over the entire storage period.
Source: Berg and Kent, 1991

7 of the 13 markets. However, in six of the seven markets, positive returns were obtained when the cost of capital is 40 percent. In Tanzania, average real price increases for maize between October and March have been 46 percent over the six-year period shown, but with one year (1990/91) accounting for half of the overall variability.

(d) Inter-seasonal price swings are sometimes a consequence of longer-term changes in market availability. Major swings in millet prices in Mali in 1990, and in maize prices in Tanzania in the same year, were not simply the effect of lean season shortages but reflected a change in the supply situation, lasting for more than a year, from one of overall grain surplus to one of scarcity. In the event of scarcity, prices tended towards an "import parity" level, i.e. prices which attract imports from neighbouring states or even from outside Africa. Conversely, in the event of surplus, they tended to fall to "export parity" level.

It is possible that food aid and the residual activities of parastatals have contributed to the flattening of inter-seasonal price curves in Sahelian countries and Tanzania. Ghana stands out in that it has never had a parastatal grain trading monopoly, notwithstanding official discouragement to inter-seasonal storage by private traders. In Tanzania price variability has been greater since 1990/91, i.e. since the formal abandonment of the parastatal marketing channel, suggesting that inter-seasonal price variability might have increased as a result of liberalization.

Legal issues

The establishment of an agricultural inventory credit programme requires a careful analysis of the existing legal framework. Among other things, this will entail a review of laws and procedures relating to the sale of goods, secured transactions, warehouse regulation, banking and credit regulation.

It should be stressed that the "practical" effects of a particular legal variable on the viability of a programme will usually not be evident from an examination of legal doctrine alone. Where the economic prospects of the scheme are strong enough, and lenders believe that the practical risks are small, then they may be able to live with a certain amount of legal ambiguity. Where, however, such prospects are not clear and the business culture of a particular country is unaccustomed to what is being proposed, legal uncertainties may present another reason for sceptical participants, particularly banks, to turn away from an uncertain venture. Thus, the development of inventory credit may require some persuasive and creative lawyering, or in the final analysis, legislative reform.

It is beyond the scope of this publication to analyse all the potential legal issues that might be encountered. In any event, these are subject to wide variation between countries. It is possible, however, to highlight some of the issues that are likely to require attention, and that may influence the way the system is set up. But even here a cautionary note is required. The following list of issues, heavily weighted toward common law jurisdictions, is not intended as exhaustive. The identification of pertinent questions in a given jurisdiction will itself vary depending upon the country being examined.

Therefore, it must be emphasized that the discussion that follows is intended as an "introduction" to some of the legal issues that may arise. It cannot be a substitute for a careful analysis of a given country's laws, which for any number of reasons may reveal significant variations on the themes presented here.

☐ **What types of security arrangements are recognized by the law of a particular country?**

The basic concept of a "security interest" is deceptively simple. Whenever a lender lends money to a borrower, the lender has a **contractual** right to the return of the money, usually with interest, in accordance with a loan agreement. This contractural right, however, is unlikely to be much use to the lender if the borrower is unable for some reason to fulfill its end of the bargain (because of insolvency, for example). Thus, the lender might require a number of additional protections as preconditions to the loan. For example, it might require that the borrower take out a certain kind of insurance or provide third-party guarantees. In a "secured lending transaction", the lender protects itself by requiring that the borrower provide collateral for the loan. This collateral might take any number of forms: land, machinery, personal possessions, inventory, receivables, etc. During the course of the loan, the lender is said to have a "security interest" in the collateral, and has rights to satisfy its debt from the collateral in the event the borrower defaults.

This simple description, of course, obscures the many nuances and frequently highly complex rules that govern secured transactions in contemporary legal systems. For example, different sets of rules often apply to different classes of collateral, the distinction between real property and personal property being one that is particularly pronounced. A host of security devices have developed over time within both common law and civil law traditions, and many more country-specific schemes are to be found on looking beyond such broad categories.

In common law systems, several types of security arrangements have evolved over the centuries. Two concepts of particular importance are the "mortgage" and the "pledge", a distinction that runs through much of the following discussion. A mortgage involves the transfer of "title" to the collateral in question.[2] In other words, in a mortgage transaction, the borrower will give to the lender a document which conveys some or all of the borrower's interest in the collateral. Usually, during the course of a mortgage loan, the borrower is entitled to keep possession of and use the collateral, and once the debt is satisfied, the title will once again revert to the borrower.

By contrast, a "pledge" agreement does not involve a transfer of title. In this type of arrangement, the lender and borrower enter into a agreement whereby certain property is pledged to the lender to secure the loan. Unlike a mortgage, a pledge requires "possession" of the object by the lender in order to perfect the security interest (see discussion of "perfection" below). In most pledge situations, the lender must actually hold the collateral in its possession. A common example may be the lender which takes physical possession of jewellery while a loan is outstanding. As we shall see, however, the concept of "constructive possession" has grown up to cover situations (such as in the case of stored grain) where it may be impossible for the lender to take actual possession of the objects in question.[3]

❑ Do a country's laws recognize a security interest in grain?

An obvious yet critical preliminary question is whether a country's legal system will **recognize** a security interest in a fungible and perishable commodity such as grain. While this cannot be taken for granted, the answer is likely to be yes, at least in common law and civil law jurisdictions.

---

[2] In some countries, the term "mortgage" has come to refer almost exclusively to secured transactions in land. For other types of property, the term "chattel mortgage" or some other terms may be used. Nevertheless, the underlying principles are the same.

[3] Through the device of "constructive possession," the practical distinction between a mortgage and a pledge can become blurred. Some legal systems have reacted to this by treating the two more or less the same. In others, however, the distinction remains something of which lawyers must be wary.

In many systems derived from Spanish civil law, the concept of a mortgage is reserved for immovable property. For other types of property, a distinction is made between a *prenda con desplazamiento* and a *prenda sin desplazamiento*. The former is akin to a typical pledge situation, in which the lender takes possession of the collateral. In the latter situation, possession remains with the borrower, and the lender obtains protection against third parties by registering notice of its interest.

Nevertheless, there may be a wide variation from country to country in the strength of this security interest, the level of protection it gives to the secured party, and the types of security arrangements that can be used, as discussed below.

□ **What level of protection will a security interest give a lender, particularly *vis-à-vis* third parties?**

To assess the strength of a particular security interest, it is important to distinguish between two relationships: the relationship of the lender to the borrower, and the relationship of the transacting parties to the outside world. The concepts of "attachment" and "perfection" – or their equivalents – which are used in many common law countries are helpful in illustrating this distinction.

When a lender and a borrower enter into an agreement using some object as security, the security interest is said to "attach" to that object. As between these two parties, the lender now has certain rights in that object if the borrower defaults on the loan. The lender may be able to take full control of the object, and sell it to satisfy the debt. But attachment alone may not be enough to protect the lender against the rights of third parties. For example, the borrower may have sold the object to someone else who did not know of the lender's security interest. This person acquires the object free of the security interest. Therefore, while the borrower is still **contractually** liable for the outstanding amount of the loan, and perhaps other damages for breaching the security agreement, the loan is now unsecured.

A "perfected" security interest does not have this weakness. Perfection occurs by some act defined by law which is deemed to give notice to the world at large that a lender has taken a security interest in particular property. Thus, when real property is being mortgaged, a specified method of registration may perfect the lender's security interest. Some form of registration may also accomplish the same thing with respect to other types of property, such as equipment, inventory or accounts. In the case of a pledge arrangement, perfection will occur where the lender takes physical (or in some cases "constructive") possession of the object during the pendancy of the loan.

Perfection gives priority to the interest of the secured party over the interests of other claimants. If a borrower has wrongfully sold property subject to a perfected security interest, the security interest remains attached to that property and the lender can still exercise its rights against the property in the event of a default.

This distinction (or similar distinctions existing in other legal traditions) is relevant to the design of inventory credit systems for several reasons. The laws of some countries, for example, explicitly provide for a system of registration by which a lender can perfect its interest in different types of mortgaged commodities. If the commodity in question is stored grain, the borrower will transfer a document evidencing title to the grain (usually a warehouse receipt, if the law recognizes it as a document of title – see below), and the lender will register this document in order to perfect its interests. This, however, is not always the case, and it is imperative that the law of each country be analysed to determine whether perfection is possible for a given type of commodity. In Ghana, for example, there is apparently no mechanism for a lender to register its interest in goods such as grain. Thus, if the borrower or the warehouse operator sells the grain to a person who is unaware of the bank's interest, the bank can no longer seize that grain to satisfy the debt.[4]

In the case of a "pledge" arrangement, the lender's possession of the collateral is usually considered sufficient to perfect its interest. In other words, the fact that a bank is holding possession of jewellry or bearer bonds is ample notice to the world at large that the bank holds a pledgee's interest in that collateral. Of course, at first glance, a pledge mechanism would not appear to be applicable to stored grain, since the bank will not have actual physical possession of the grain. However, many jurisdictions recognize the concept of "constructive possession," whereby a lender can rely upon documentary proof that the person who has physical custody of the property is acting on its behalf. For this purpose, a warehouse receipt transferred to

---

[4] Given that sold grain is likely to be hard to track down anyway, the comfort provided by the fact that a security interest "follows" the grain may be largely illusory. More important is that the lender's rights might not be given priority in the event the borrower goes bankrupt or dies.

the bank by the depositor will be valuable. However, the bank will almost always want explicit acknowledgement from the warehouse owner that the grain is now being held on behalf of the bank. This is often known as an "attornment" agreement.[5] A collateral management agreement between lender, borrower and warehouse typically contains such attornment language. Annex 3 contains an example of such an agreement used in Ghana.

☐ **Do a country's laws recognize a warehouse receipt as a "document of title" to the grain evidenced by that receipt?**

The potential role of warehouse receipts has already been alluded to in the preceding discussion of mortgages/pledges and attachment/perfection. The attractiveness of a warehouse receipt as a mechanism for securing credit hinges in part on whether national law recognizes it as a "transferable document of title" (or something which is conceptually similar, although given a different label in different legal traditions). This is in fact two questions: is the receipt a "document of title" and, if so, is it "transferable"? The first question is dealt with here; the question of transferability, including the narrower concept of "negotiability", will be discussed under the next heading.

A document of title is a document that, by law or by business custom, is generally considered sufficient evidence that the person to whom the document is issued has title to the property it describes. Such documents typically include bills of lading, for example.

It will be recalled that a mortgage-type arrangement conceptually involves the transfer of "title" to the collateral between borrower and lender. Therefore, for designing stored grain credit systems, a critical question will be whether warehouse receipts are treated under applicable law as documents of title. In some countries, the law explicitly recognizes warehouse receipts as title documents. This is true, for example, in India and the US. In others, this might not be the case. Some countries, for example, might

---

[5] Where negotiable warehouse receipts are involved, an attornment by the warehouse operator is technically not necessary, since the warehouse receipt itself will state on its face that the operator has a duty to whoever the holder might be. Even so, a bank may want some explicit acknowledgement of its rights by the warehouse for additional protection.

simply treat warehouse receipts as evidence of **possession** of the stored grain by the warehouse operator on behalf of the depositer. In such situations, a mere transfer and registration of the receipt may not be sufficient to give the lender security. Instead, it may be necessary to resort to a "constructive pledge" arrangement, involving the attornment of the warehouse owner (see above for discussion of "constructive pledge" and "attornment").[6]

❏ Is a warehouse receipt a transferable and negotiable instrument?

In order for a warehouse receipt to be useful with stored grain, it will be essential for the receipt to be "transferable". In other words, there must be nothing in the law or on the face of the document that prevents the borrower from transferring his rights under the receipt to the lender.

A transferable receipt may also be subject to a further distinction in some legal systems: is it a non-negotiable or negotiable instrument? Sometimes the concepts of "transferability" and "negotiability" are blurred together: when a borrower transfers a document to a lender in exchange for a loan, it would seem that the document has been negotiated. Thus, the terms "transferable" and "negotiable" are frequently used interchangeably.

However, in some legal systems negotiability is a more specialized concept than simply the ability to transfer the document. A negotiable instrument in such systems is not only transferable, but confers upon the transferee a direct interest in the underlying property free of any outstanding claims. For example, the holder of a negotiable receipt would be entitled to the goods as described in the document, whatever the depositor or the

---

[6] The form of the document issued by the warehouse may also affect whether it is treated as a document of title. Much litigation in the US has focused on the difference between a formal warehouse receipt and a simple scale ticket indicating only that a certain amount of a particular type of grain was delivered to the warehouse. Many farmers are content to accept the latter. However, since this document does not clearly define the legal positions of the depositer and the warehouse, it can lead to ambiguity later on. Has the farmer retained title to the grain which is now in the possession of the warehouse? Or was it the intention of the parties that the warehouse take title, subject to its obligation to pay the farmer for the grain at some later date (usually upon sale to an outside purchaser)? Obviously, this distinction is of great importance to a bank lending against the grain.

warehouse operator may have done to the goods in the meantime. By contrast, the rights of the transferee of a non-negotiable receipt will be equivalent to the rights of the transferor. Thus, the transferee may find that its rights have been defeated by the sale of the grain to a good faith purchaser. It will be noted that when "negotiability" is used in this sense, the transferee of a negotiable receipt may actually acquire rights **superior** to those that the transferor had at the time of transfer. This may seem somewhat counter-intuitive, but the purpose of such a rule is to facilitate a market in such documents in which purchasers, often far removed from the underlying goods and the original transaction, can rely upon what the document says.

Thus, from the perspective of a lender who is holding a receipt as security, its characterization as a negotiable document of title is attractive for several reasons. It gives the lender all the rights of the original depositor (and perhaps more) with respect to the deposited grain, upon presentation of the receipt to the warehouse operator. The warehouse operator is duty bound to release the goods only to the holder of the receipt, even with no prior knowledge of to whom the document has been transferred. In the event of a default by the borrower, the lender can simply sell the receipt in order to liquidate the collateral, instead of having first to take physical possession of the grain. Negotiability is also an important precondition for the emergence of a secondary market in such loans, and gives the lender greater flexibility with respect to its loan portfolio.

Some national laws make explicit provisions for negotiable warehouse receipts. Under the Warehouse Acts passed by various states in India, for example, warehouse receipts are transferable by endorsement, unless otherwise stated on the receipt itself. Warehousing laws and the Uniform Commercial Code in the US have also established a system of negotiable warehouse receipts. The laws of many civil law countries also contain similar provisions. In Nicaragua, for example, *certificados de depósito* can be *negociable* instruments (although here it appears that negotiability is closer conceptually to free transferability, without the specialized meaning found in many common law jurisdictions).

In many countries, however, such clear statutory provisions are lacking. An analysis of Ghanaian law, for example, has concluded that there is no law which accords the status of negotiable documents of title to warehouse receipts. By contrast, other documents that are generally regarded as negotiable in Ghana, e.g. promissory notes or bills of exchange, have had that status spelled out in legislation.[7] In such ambiguous situations, some legislative intervention will probably be necessary if the eventual goal is a system of freely tradeable warehouse receipts.

Again, it is important to recognize that a non-negotiable warehouse receipt may still be useful for credit purposes. In simple loan arrangements where both the borrower and the warehouse are well known to the bank, and where the easy transferability of the loan on the secondary market is not a high priority, a non-negotiable receipt may be sufficient. If a non-negotiable receipt is "transferable" and a "document of title," it can still be used as a way for a borrower to grant to the lender an interest in the underlying goods in a mortgage-style transaction. And even where a warehouse receipt is not recognized as a document of title, it might be used in connection with a pledge arrangement to show that the bank has "constructive possession" of the collateral.

☐ Can an effective security interest be given in goods which are commingled as part of an undifferentiated bulk?

In some warehouses, grain from numerous depositers is commingled. A depositor is thus entitled to delivery of a certain amount of grain rather than to the **actual** grain deposited. A critical question is whether the depositor can give an effective security interest to a bank in such a situation.

The answer to this question is sometimes riddled with ambiguities. In England, for example, under the Sale of Goods Act 1979, the purchaser of a specified quantity of a bulk of goods is not deemed to have acquired title to those goods until the portion that he or she has purchased is actually identified and differentiated from the rest of the bulk. By extension, this might raise questions about whether a bank's security interest can be said to attach to an undifferentiated right to a portion of a bulk. In England, the

---

[7]Indeed, it is a general rule in English common law that "negotiability" of a particular type of instrument cannot simply be declared by the parties to that instrument. Negotiability must be determined either by law or by long-established custom.

courts have construed the Sale of Goods Act to mean that a "mortgage" of undifferentiated goods is not possible. This is because, as already discussed, a mortgage involves a transfer of "title". It would be impossible for a borrower to transfer title to undifferentiated grain if it cannot be said he or she had title to it in the first place. However, even in England, it is possible in such situations for the borrower to enter into a "pledge" agreement.

Of course, such an issue will not arise where the grain of individual depositors is stored separately and in readily identifiable lots. Furthermore, the issue generally does not arise in civil law systems, which have on the whole taken a more pragmatic approach to the question of undifferentiated bulks.

❐ Does the legal personality of the borrower have an effect on the lender's security?

This question is of critical importance for lenders. In many countries, the ability of different types of borrowers to enter into particular types of secured loan depends upon their legal "personality." In other words, different rules may apply if the borrower is an individual, a partnership, an unincorporated association, or a company. Many common law countries make it easy for companies to register a charge, while making it extremely difficult for individuals to do the same. In some jurisdictions, it is legally impossible for a partnership or unincorporated association to engage in any secured transactions. Obviously, this is relevant for a programme that targets mainly farmers and small traders who are unlikely to be incorporated

Annex 3

Specimen collateral management agreement

NOTA BENE: This is an example of a document in use in Ghana, and is not meant for universal application.

COLLATERAL MANAGEMENT AGREEMENT

THIS AGREEMENT is made the _____ day of _____ 1994
Among: _____   _____
 (hereinafter called the "Depositor")

OF THE FIRST PART

and: _____ a company/partnership existing
 under the laws of Ghana and having its principal place of business situate
 at _____ , Accra in the Greater-Accra Region of the
 Republic of Ghana (hereinafter called "the Collateral Manager")

OF THE SECOND PART

and: _____ XYZ BANK LIMITED, a bank
 formed under the laws of Ghana having its Registered Office situate at
 Accra aforesaid (hereinafter called the "Bank")

OF THE THIRD PART

Whereas:

(1) The Depositor is the owner of maize (hereinafter called the "Commodities").

(2) The Bank has agreed to grant a credit facility to the Depositor secured by a pledge on the Commodities.

(3) The Depositor and the Bank wish the Collateral Manager to handle and store the Commodities for the account of the Bank, and the Collateral

Manager has agreed to do so upon the terms and conditions mentioned hereinafter.

NOW THIS AGREEMENT WITNESSES that in pursuance of the premises and in consideration of the mutual understandings and agreements herein contained the parties hereto HAVE AGREED as follows:

1. **Appointment:** The Depositor hereby appoints the Collateral Manager who accepts to receive the Commodities for storage and handling for the benefit of the Bank according to the terms hereinafter provided and the Collateral Manager Warehousing General Terms and Conditions attached hereto as Annex I[8] which forms a part hereof.

2. **Warehouse:** The Commodities shall be stored in a warehouse situated at _____ .

3. **Description of services:** The Collateral Manager shall render the following services:

   - *Receipt of Commodities*
   (a) The Collateral Manager shall receive the Commodities at the door of the warehouse and unload them using casual labourers specially hired for this purpose.
   (b) Once discharged from the trucks, the Collateral Manager will stack the Commodities in the warehouse in an appropriate manner and in accordance with the local regulations for maize. At that stage, the Collateral Manager will prepare a report for each truck and will fill stack cards for each lot.
   (c) If requested, the Collateral Manager will perform a 100 percent weighing control and a quality classification of the Commodities, by analysing a representative sample of each lot, according to the specifications which will be agreed upon by the parties.
   (d) Within 48 hours of receipt of the Commodities into store (excluding Sundays and public holidays) the Collateral Manager will notify the parties by fax of the details of the consignment received.

---

[8]Not attached here

(e) After confirmation received from the Bank the Collateral Manager will issue a Warehouse Receipt to the Bank in the form attached hereto as Annex II[9] which forms a part hereof.

- *Storage of Commodities*

(f) The Collateral Manager will store the goods in the warehouse until delivery as provided hereunder.

- *Delivery of Commodities*

(g) Upon advice from the Bank of an expected date of delivery of the Commodities from the Warehouse with all the necessary information the Collateral Manager will prepare the lot to be delivered.

(h) If requested the Collateral Manager will fumigate the Commodities before delivery.

(i) When a delivery is programmed the Collateral Manager will arrange the delivery of the Commodities ex warehouse and ensure that all the bags which have been prepared are taken for loading into the respective wagons. These manoeuvres will also be done by casual labourers hired for this purpose by the Collateral Manager and, if requested, the Collateral Manager will also perform a spot weight checking at this stage.

(j) The Collateral Manager will arrange loading and proper storage of the Commodities on the wagons and, if requested, will also seal these wagons.

(k) The Collateral Manager shall ensure that the Commodities to be delivered correspond with the specifications stated on the Warehouse Receipt(s) handed over by the Bank.

(l) Upon completion of delivery, the Collateral Manager will issue a report of delivery and/or certificate of delivery per lot delivered, in accordance with the instructions of the Bank, specifying the quantity of bags and other relevant details of the lot. The Collateral Manager will also take possession of the original document issued by the Railways or other transporter once the Bank has given to the Railways

---

[9]See Annex 4 page 105

or other Transporter the necessary delivery instructions confirming delivery and will immediately courier these documents to the Bank.

4. **Release of Commodities:** For greater certainty it is hereby stated and agreed that the Collateral Manager shall not allow the release of any Commodities unless it has received written instructions from the Bank stating the person to whom the Commodities shall be released and the date and manner of such release, notwithstanding alternative or contradictory instructions from the Depositor.

5. **Insurance:** The Depositor will arrange for an all-risks policy or such other policy or policies as the Bank shall determine to cover the Commodities.

6. **Commingling of Commodities:** All Commodities stored hereunder may be commingled and warehoused as one general lot of fungible goods and the Bank shall be entitled to such portion of such general lot as the amount of the Commodity represented by the Warehouse Receipt bears to the whole of such general lot of such Commodities.

7. **Fees:** In consideration of the services provided by the Collateral Manager herein, the Bank will pay the Collateral Manager the following fees for its services:

   (a) receipt and delivery of Commodities as per Section 3(a), (b), (d), (g), (i) to (l): Cedi ___ per tonne;

   (b) storage of Commodities as per Section 3(f): Cedi ___ per tonne per fortnight or part thereof;

   (c) insurance, if any, as per Section 5: 0, _% per month based on the value of the Commodities stored in the warehouse on the first day of each month;

   (d) issue of warehouse receipt as per Section 3(e) and other sundry costs: Cedi ___ per tonne.

   Notwithstanding the above the Bank agrees to pay the Collateral Manager a minimum monthly fee of Cedi ___ .

8. **Other Charges:** The fees mentioned in Section 7 do not include the services mentioned in Section 3(c) and (h) or other services which shall be charged under a separate agreement among the parties.

9. **Payments:** All fees will be charged monthly by the Collateral Manager and the Bank will pay same within 30 days of the date of issue of the Collateral Manager's invoice. Payments of fees made by the Bank hereunder shall be debited to the Depositor's account with the Bank for reimbursement accordingly.

10. **Access to Commodities:** Apart from employees, agents or contractors of the Collateral Manager, the Collateral Manager will only admit persons to the warehouse who have been so authorized by the Bank.

11. **Indemnity:** In consideration of the Collateral Manager agreeing to act in accordance with the instructions of the Bank, the Depositor undertakes to indemnify the Collateral Manager and to keep it fully indemnified against all losses, damages, costs and expenses incurred or sustained by the Collateral Manager whatsoever nature and howsoever arising out of or in connection with such instructions of the Bank, provided the Collateral Manager acts in good faith. Further, the Collateral Manager shall not be liable for any action taken or omitted by it under or in connection with the instructions of the Bank.

12. **Lien:** Nothing herein shall restrict or negate any lien or other rights that the Collateral Manager may have on the Commodities. The parties expressly agree that the Collateral Manager's licence shall rank *pari passu* with the pledge or security given by the Depositor to the Bank.

13. **Duration:** This Agreement comes into force on the date of its execution and will terminate upon 30 days' notice by a party to the others.

14. **Holding-on period:** In case of termination by a party as provided in Section 13 the Collateral Manager shall continue to hold the Commodities until such time as the Bank notifies the Collateral Manager of the name of the person to whom, and the place where, the Collateral Manager shall deliver the Commodities. If such person and place are not designated within 60 days of the date of termination of this Agreement the Collateral Manager may sell the Commodities in accordance with Annex I.

15. **Amendments:** This Agreement shall not be changed or supplemented in any way except by properly executed documents signed by a representative or officer duly authorized in writing by each of the parties hereto.

16. **Assignments:** Except as expressly provided herein, any assignment of this Agreement or any right hereunder by any of the parties hereto without the prior written consent of the other parties shall be null and void.

17. **Arbitration:** It is hereby agreed and understood that the parties hereto shall carry out this Agreement in the spirit of mutual co-operation and good faith and that any difference, dispute or controversies shall be resolved and settled amicably among the parties hereto. If, however, amicable settlement shall not be possible, the parties hereto agree that all questions or differences whatsoever which may at any time hereafter arise between the parties hereto or their respective representatives touching this agreement or the subject matter thereof or arising out of or in relation thereto respectively and whether as to construction or otherwise shall be referred to a single arbitrator in case the parties can agree upon one otherwise to two arbitrators one to be appointed by each party to the difference whether consisting of more than one person or not and in either case in accordance with and subject to the provisions of the Arbitration Acts, 1961 (Act 38) or any then subsisting statutory modification thereof.

18. **Conflict with Annex I:** In case of conflict between the provisions of this Agreement and Annex I the former shall prevail.

19. **Applicable Law:** This Agreement shall be construed and interpreted in accordance with the laws of Ghana.

IN WITNESS whereof the parties have executed this Agreement on the date first above written.

SIGNED SEALED AND DELIVERED
by: _____
on behalf of the: _____
(the Depositor)
herein the presence of:_____

SIGNED SEALED AND DELIVERED
by: _____
on behalf of the: _____
(the Collateral Manager)
 herein the presence of: _____

SIGNED SEALED AND DELIVERED
by: _____
on behalf of the: _____
(the Bank)
 herein the presence of: _____

Annex 4

Specimen warehouse receipt

NOTA BENE: This is an example of a document proposed for use in Ghana, and is not meant for universal application.

WAREHOUSE RECEIPT NO. ____

ISSUED TO: _____ XYZ BANK REF. OF COLLATERAL MANAGER

This is to certify that the undersigned has received the following goods for storage in apparent good order and condition (except as noted) subject to the Collateral Manager Warehousing General Terms and Conditions and the Collateral Management Agreement between the Collateral Managers, XYZ Bank and _____ dated_____1994

MARKS & NUMBERS	DESCRIPTION OF GOODS	REMARKS/NOTES

GROSS WEIGHT:	kg	NET WEIGHT:	kg
NO. OF PACKAGES:		DATE RECEIVED:	
LOCATION OF STORAGE:		WAREHOUSE RENT:	

INSURANCE:

This Warehouse Receipt is not a negotiable document of title and therefore does not evidence title to the goods mentioned herein. It cannot be negotiated nor used as collateral security.

Delivery or partial delivery of the goods will only be made upon written instructions from XYZ Bank in accordance with the Collateral Management Agreement above-stated.

The undersigned is not responsible for the contents or description of the goods.

THE COLLATERAL MANAGER

DATE: _____   _____

References

BERG, E. and KENT, L. (1991) *The Economics of Cereal Banks in the Sahel*. Consultancy report prepared for USAID by Development Associates Inc., Bethesda, Maryland.

BOXALL, P.A. and BICKERSTETH, J.S. (1991) *Liberalization of Cereals Marketing in Sub-Saharan Africa: Implementation Issues*. Report No. 3: *Ghana – A Case Study*. Chatham, UK: Natural Resources Institute. (unpublished).

COULTER, J.P. (1993) The Malian experience in financing the cereals trade. *African Review of Money Finance and Banking*, 1: 27-45.

COULTER, J.P. (1994) *Liberalization of Cereals Marketing in Sub-Saharan Africa: Lessons from Experience*. Marketing Series 9. Chatham, UK: Natural Resources Institute.

COULTER, J.P. and GOLOB, P. (1992) Cereal marketing liberalization in Tanzania. In: *Food Policy*, December: 420-430.

MARKETING DEVELOPMENT BUREAU (1992) *The Wholesale Trade in Grains and Beans in Tanzania*. Dar es Salaam: Marketing Development Bureau. 77pp.

TROTTER, B.W. (1992) *Applying Price Analysis to Marketing Systems: Methods and Examples from the Indonesian Rice Market*. Marketing Series 3. Chatham: Natural Resources Institute.

WORLD BANK (1991) *Ghana, Medium-Term Agricultural Development Strategy (MTADS); an Agenda for Sustained Growth and Development (1991-2000)*. Vol. 1. Report no. 8914-GH. Washington, DC: World Bank.

FAO TECHNICAL PAPERS

FAO AGRICULTURAL SERVICES BULLETINS

Availability: September 1995

Ar	–	Arabic	Multil –	Multilingual
C	–	Chinese	*	Out of print
E	–	English	* *	In preparation
F	–	French		
P	–	Portuguese		
S	–	Spanish		

The FAO Technical Papers are available through the authorized FAO Sales Agents or directly from Distribution and Sales Section, FAO, Viale delle Terme di Caracalla, 00100 Rome, Italy.